# TOM
# POSTELL

## On the Life and Work
## of an American Master

ISBN: 978-1-7344356-4-1

Published by Unsung Masters Series in collaboration with *Gulf Coast,*
*Cincinnati Review, Copper Nickel,* and *Pleiades.*

Department of English
University of Houston
Houston, TX 77204

Produced at the University of Houston Department of English

Distributed by Small Press Distribution (SPD) and to subscribers
of *Cincinnati Review, Copper Nickel, Pleiades: Literature in Context* and
*Gulf Coast: A Journal of Literature and Fine Arts.*

Series, cover, and interior design by Martin Rock.
Cover photograph of unknown origin, likely a postal personnel ID.
Courtesty of the Postell/Jones family.

2  4  6  8  9  7  5  3  1
First Printing, 2024

The Unsung Masters Series brings the work of great, out-of-print,
little-known writers to new readers. Each volume in the Series
includes a large selection of the author's original writing, as well as
essays on the writer, interviews with people who knew the writer,
photographs, and ephemera. The curators of the Unsung Masters
Series are always interested in suggestions for future volumes.

Invaluable financial support for this project
provided by the University of Houston English Department.

# UNIVERSITY of **HOUSTON**

# TOM POSTELL

## On the Life and Work of an American Master

Edited by MICHAEL C. PETERSON
and ANTHONY SUTTON

ADDITIONAL TITLES AVAILABLE AT

# unsungmasters.org

# THE UNSUNG MASTERS SERIES

**gULF COASt**

A JOURNAL OF LITERATURE AND FINE ARTS

············································· IN COLLABORATION WITH ·······································

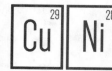

# CONTENTS

## INTRODUCTION

MICHAEL C. PETERSON

## POEMS

## Uncollected Poems (1950–1980)

## CONVERSATIONS

# LINER NOTES

Tom with his cat Rain, 1975.
Photo courtesy of Rose Bianchi.

# INTRODUCTION:
# A RIMSHOT FOR TOM POSTELL

## Michael C. Peterson

> *Drumming is martial art*
> —Fred Moten

Turning off Mound Street will take you into the heart of poet Tom Postell's birthplace: Cincinnati's West End, the historic and perpetually rocked cradle of Black culture and capital, where he lived from 1927 to 1952. The massive rhomboid footprint of the long-since demolished Laurel Homes and Lincoln Court federal housing projects are only traceable now by feeling around its edge in a series of hard rights on spaced-out reds. The Regal Theater and Linn business district remain, enjambed by a new stadium and townhouses built to look bygone. Tom's earliest home on Findlay is a palisade of bricked-up renaissance revival. Armory Street, his last point of contact, is still off John but has been renamed. New streets, like consonant strings, are just versions of the old: shifted left or right maybe by matters of feet. Little shift, city planners said. Not far off and over the Ohio, Roebling first erected his Brooklyn Bridge: a trial-run, a simulacrum now for the realer thing. Insert the joke about everything getting to Cincinnati twenty years late.

I've driven here to think about Tom again, to see if I can't play some of the notes right. UDF coffee. Black licorice from Aglamesis. Half past midnight in a car looking southbound from the corner of Mound and East Ninth as westbound traffic flashes by as if on rails, aiming for outlet or interchange to any freedom from Downtown's mulish one-ways. Liberty or Ezzard Charles, the arteries that will always carry you in or out. I'm trying to look beyond a new commercial property's empty lot and through some double-ranked elms planted to hide the interstate's huge concrete volutes. Perfect trees from the civil-engineering catalogue of trees. Behind them, two city blocks south and sixty years ago would have stood the Cotton Club, a doppelganger of Harlem's one-and-the-same, the first integrated jazz venue of the Queen City. The Sterling Hotel. Cordelia's down the way. Haven and hiring rail of a touring Ellington, Sarah Vaughn, or Basie. To get any closer to the exact spot tonight would mean standing in a northbound lane of I75. The city's 1958 prerogative to "slum clear" the so-called Kenyon-Barr decimated the last of the West End's ligature through the Rat and Sausage Rows to the river. The Cotton Club at 6th and Mound shuttered in 1955, the same year Charlie Parker died.

Like Parker and the West End both, Tom Postell was an artist gone too soon. A cipher of a poet, associated with the New

York Beat Generation and Black Arts Movements of the 1950's and 60's, Postell's silhouette has been but lightly sketched by literary historians, though his impact on his coevals is the stuff of poetry folkways. He ran contemporaneous with both the canonical (Amiri Baraka, Sonia Sanchez, Jayne Cortez, Ishmael Reed) and the more recently recovered Lorenzo Thomas, Henry Dumas, and Calvin Hernton—names we've now come to recognize not as outlying but core to the period. While he isn't repped by the era's emergent Black anthologies, scholar Aldon Lynn Nielson points out his few publications "indicate that he was a poet of considerable interest, poised to make a significant contribution to the aesthetics of Black verse." His presumed death (or disappearance) and unavailing papertrail have left poets and scholars wishing for his reemergence.

And yet, even armed with new evidence, there's a resistance to looking for Tom, let alone locking down his guileful rhythms and kooky insolence. He reads decidedly subjunctive—a haunted voice wishing after its own haunting possibilities—and he's likewise keen to misdirect, to version himself according to those wishes' needs. "To tell the truth / repeatedly requires a sense of the lie," he writes in a poem titled simply "Poem." In another: "to remove a sly wonder from a plain dissatisfaction a lie must tutor a lie." Postell's instinct to float through the era's discordant spaces—to radicalize romantic sentiment with "sly wonder" wooing chaos—is crucial to his appeal. We love a saboteur for his dissatisfaction, his combo of impact and anonymity. Much of Postell's story still feels renegade. To "catch it" as he writes, we may have *to play it outside*, as Max Roach would say.

Thomas "Tee" Postell was born Thomas Freeman Postell Jr. on August 7th, 1927. He and two sisters, Pauline and Katherine, were raised in the redlined West End of Cincinnati, Ohio. Postell's father Thomas Freeman Postell

Sr. worked as a Pullman porter, a desirable and respected job that enabled his family to stay out of the coldwater flats many Black families were afforded at the time. His mother, Maud, ran the household—no small feat given the frequent, long-range shifts of her husband. His sister, Katherine Postell, though ninety-seven years-old at the time of this publication, recalls a house full of horn music, summers in the cool dark of the Regal Theater, and walks to gather the small pears from community orchards of Lower Price Hill. Much of the family's attention turned to Postell Sr. in 1940, when a dogged tuberculosis forced the patriarch into his final nine years in the Dunham Sanitarium.

According to Katherine, Tom likely began writing poetry while a student at Hughes High School, but a near-physical conflict with a teacher spurred him to leave for naval enlistment with just two years of high school under his belt. Postell's draft DSS-1 indicates he likely lied about his birthdate, allowing him to enlist in 1944 at just seventeen. He was promptly deployed to a staging center at Pearl Harbor just before war's end, with an honorable discharge as third-class gunner's mate in 1946.

To the consternation of the household, Tom returned to Cincinnati with a silver-pearl Ludwig drumkit, likely purchased on his receiving route back through San Francisco. "He'd beat on that thing 'til it drove us all crazy," opines Katherine. "And I remember this—Tee loved *rimshots* as he called'em. He was always working on his rimshots. *Thwap!*—like that. Loud as all get-out." Indeed, one can hear the slanged snare rolls and tomtom fills that generate the stop-time of early poems like "The Young Know the Old Are Dead":

Whip who
to what shit
better start to run
to stop
ending
on a hang up.

Whip which
sprung
ideas
I told a long time ago

ending
on a hang up.

"If not overtly jazz we might even sense a residue of military cadence here, something like drum and fife rhythm, longer lines ("I told a long time ago") swirling over a shorter percussive backdrop. Postell's service aligns with many of his peers' born in the era (Baraka, John A. Williams, Dudley Randall, Ray Durem, Etheridge Knight), as does his educational arc which sees him accrue some years of college post-discharge. The GI Bill benefitted a non-southern Black veteran like Postell moreso, but only by a margin, and, like many, Tom never finished the degree he sought (a BA in Economics). Nor did Tom seem to maintain much relation thereafter to the academic circles that would become new footholds for the radical political poetries of the late sixties and seventies. After leaving school sometime around 1948 he worked as a copywriter, ad salesman, and studio engineer at Radio WNOP in Newport (later reborn as the famous floating Jazz Ark of the Ohio) and apprenticing under Ernie Waits, the tri-state's first African American disc-jockey and noted civil rights leader. A second enlistment came in 1950, this time with a service barge stationed on Lake Michigan. His Naval 601 paperwork notes "writing poetry as a leisure time activity" and time aboard the YR-51—an at-the-ready live/work support vessel not unlike the Naval version of a jazz sideman—would have given him time to do just that. After just over a year, Postell was moved to reserve and returned to Cincinnati, then Dayton (we have just one draft of one poem from this address), before what would be his momentous move to New York City sometime in 1953 or 1954.

It's in this emigration to the Lower East Side that we begin to locate Postell within the maximum bohemia of post-war American poetry and, more significantly, a co-incident Black avant-gardism that sees racial disambiguation and liberation as central to its praxis. It's also in these formative years that he produces the primary finished manuscript we editors are left with: a book of poems titled *Poems from the Tomb*. Scholars lose the trail of Postell in this move, though his sister Katherine's memory—which we are profoundly fortunate and honored to present in this volume—illumines facets of Tom's life during this most ambitious period. This decade and a half between 1953 and 1969 would be Postell's most productive and focused, though we have little but the poems to account for it. The lone substantial literary record of Postell's modus comes to us via Amiri Baraka, an account that serves both to inaugurate and, unfortunately, delimit Postell in a number of critical ways.

In his 1969 collection *Black Magic*, Baraka, great impresario of the Black Arts Movement—what Larry Neal calls the "artistic arm of the Black Power Movement"—would publish a book that remains a kind of contrafact of how we try to tell a more complex story of midcentury Black activism. Dated between 1965 and 1966, "For Tom Postell, Dead Black Poet" first appears publicly in this volume, just over a year before Baraka's monumental call-to-arms of "It's Nation

One of the last photos of Tom, with sister Katherine,
wife Rose, and family. Christmas, 1979.
Photo courtesy of Postell/Jones Family.

Time" at the 1970 Congress of African Peoples in Atlanta.
"For Tom Postell" sits astride poems like "The Black Man
is Making New Gods" and "Sacred Chant for the Return
of Black Spirit and Power." These poems ratify what Black
Arts sees as the necessary spiritual evolution of the period:
from a poetry obedient to what Dudley Randall dubbed the
"obscure Greenwich Village idiom" of white Beat, Black
Mountain, and New York School contemporaries, toward one
of a vaulting Black space requiring the razing of that idiom.
In its place—not just a page but a space acoustically expansive
and spiritual—would be a new embodied vernacular of Black
Nationalism for a post-segregationist era. Baraka's poems
stoke controversy, with "For Tom Postell, Dead Black Poet"

one of the taller lightning rods for discussion of Baraka's anti-Semitism, homophobia, or essentialized Black rage.

Wide as the discourse has become, you won't come up short if you google the poem's title and let the algorithm work. You *will* come up short on the elegy's "dead" man, however—a poet we now know to be still very much alive at the time of Baraka's composition in 1965. Curiously, 1965 was also the year Baraka published his essay "Raise, Race, Rays, Raze," electing Postell one the era's "new masters"—what he terms the "First ('primitive') and next ('modern') phase" of Black work. Yet the search results always reenact the eulogy. Already, meager information about Postell is available; as his peers pass, we're losing what's left of the oral record. Or: Postell's few publications result in little evidence of his presence in poetry networks as data-mapped. What statements, even as cursory searches of poets once considered "cult," "marginal," or "outsider" can now—given the faceted digital archive, always updating—lead curious readers into deep-dives that baffle with their glimmering copia. Searching for a living, vibrant Postell makes digging after some of his similarly overlooked contemporaries feel like light work. Undersung Black innovators we might cite as cases in crypsis—Stephen Jonas, Harrold Carrington, N.H. Pritchard—are coming to be truly dug again in the way they deserve. Jonas, in particular, indexes well with Postell: both were deep-reading autodidacts, romantics in league with their own mythos, east-coast transplants with ancestral ties to Georgia.

Like Baraka, Postell can be viewed as a bridge figure of America's Black avant-garde in the fifties and sixties, and what poems survive from him have been passionately curated by just a handful of indomitable editors. Lauri Scheyer and Aldon Lynn Nielson's *Every Goodbye Ain't Gone* is an indispensable guidebook to these complex decades, and gives us the only close-readings of Postell's technical prowess; Franklin Rosemont and Robin D.G. Kelley's *Black, Brown, & Beige* restores Postell to an illuminating heritage of diasporic surrealism stretching from Africa to the Caribbean. These editors have done the hardest work to identify Postell, who otherwise remains a ghost-note in the polyrhythms of the period.

"We must also account for the period's predominantly White editorship: not merely its failure to give Postell's work its due "home" (as it failed so many others), but its active fugitivization of such work, aside even from any avant-garde bona fides. "Paper is white but the ink is black / . . . I propose a black editor in every poet's pot comes my new world," writes Postell in "Opus 31" sometime in the Spring of 1975. In the same poem just seven lines later this utopic vision turns back upon itself: "My buds bloom no more I've turned them inward seeking a home." There certainly is, to comp with theorist Saidiya Hartman, a waywardness to Postell's work. The archive lives to reject this, marked as his art is with errantry, with what Hartman calls the "ambience and minor music" of Black life. Publishing prejudice enforces decades and centuries of archival dispossession and violence in exactly this way. We can read the emotional impact in many of Postell's poems: part of his very insurgency is that he throws so much language and thinking at the problem: to the void lurking behind rejection, outsideness, and invisibility. There's almost a prophetic sense that this void will feel the same as any literary "belonging" might—a sense of eulogy always native to the thinking. That said, this eulogic feeling may actually be autonomy.

Partnering, communing, and carousing were fundamental to Tom's character. His niece Beverly Miller remembers him as the funny and "cool-talking" uncle. Yet *connectedness* in his poems is often existentially married to happenstance, pining, and hiccup. In "Poem [voice of void]" he maps a romantic encounter. Coolness, of a variety, is central to its register:

> voice of void girl jams the concert tubes of thought.
> air turns back into the room and breathes autumn, doldrums.
> girl smiles or doesn't smile, she wanders idly by.
> love has ridden astray on an eagle's back, happiness clings to a memory, one thinks
> in the evening after a ringing hell-bell day, lights drown the room, sighing.
> how beautiful can love and girl be? when does the line draw itself.

Even in doldrum, Postell's poems wing on imagery as if riding a self-made thermal—sails generating their own wind. With lines stretching to 22 syllables and anywhere between 7 and 10 beats per line, this poem is a clinic on lyric stamina, the poet pushing ever-further into an almost philosophical question about what an encounter (or even the *thinking* of an encounter) might mean. If this is a blues with a blues-temporality—one that allows Postell's lovers to cross space-time into a moment of honest romantic appraisal—then it's a surreal, maximalist blues flirting with a total dissolution. Memory, mythos, season, and sound are let in to multiply the moment, but the poet's brinksmanship is kept cleverly in check by his own pace and punctuation. The sighing sentiment ("how beautiful can love and girl be") could be almost Victorian, were it not for Postell's syncopations of image and phrase. The speaker *might* actually want an answer—but resignation is almost preferable as it lets question beat on infinitely.

Poems like this reveal a fusion of three of Postell's core poetry chakras: surrealism, jazz, and the eye of the flâneur. Amiri Baraka corroborates these qualities in Tom, both as a person and an artist. Scholars like Scheyer and Nielsen posit—and we believe our work confirms—that Postell appears under pseudonym as "Tim Poston" in the *Autobiography of LeRoi Jones* (1981):

> He was also a poet, older than the rest of us. He'd been influenced by surrealists of one kind or another, and he was kinda wiggy anyway. At the time I knew him he, he had already (unlike most of us) developed a distinctive style— surreal, cynical, and funny, just like him . . . . I liked him I guess because he was a *real* poet. He had a surety to his hand . . . . Tim was out, he was on the fringe of everything. It was [Tom] who hipped me to the dangerous state of race relations in the Village. (Baraka 132)

The legit bohemian some seven years older than Baraka, Postell fits the drift of the *Autobiography's* sardonic Virgil-figure here. A dated draft of one of Postell's quintessential "city" poems from 1953 may put his arrival in NYC at roughly four years prior to Baraka's in 1957. His apartment, recalled by sister Katherine Jones to be on both 6th and 9th Streets during two phases of his Manhattan residency roughly aligns with Baraka's noting its proximity to the Cooper Union. Hearing the description of Tee's apartment, a small, wild cell of a room awash with typewritten papers, books, and empty bottles, Katherine nods and laughs: "He let me up only once—it was a wreck—never let me up again."

Postell shows up in only two other slivers of documentation from the period. In a 1975 interview with Skip Gates, Ted Joans (who famously boarded with one of Postell's

Black Naval Reserve unit (Postell pictured upper right)
aboard receiving vessel, Pearl Harbor or San Francisco, c. 1945.
Photo courtesy of Postell/Jones Family.

heroes, Charlie Parker, across the street from the Café Bohemia in the early fifties) namechecks Postell as both an associate and influence: "He was a beat generation poet like the rest of us. I never saw a black beatnik, though. Black poets read to beatniks; the people who lay out in cafes were labelled beatniks." But perhaps more fascinating is yet another poem in Postell's honor courtesy of E.O. Kean (Edwin O. Kean), a fellow Village poet born in the U.S. Virgin Islands and page-neighbor to Postell in *Yugen*'s first 1958 issue. Kean's short but long-lined "The Way I Want To (For Tom Postell)" appears in the seminal Beat journal *Beatitude* (17: 1961) and steals a little something of Tom's cadence in homage:

> In gothic, modern, and storefront, the godly continue their
> lying
> And nobody else will be saved
> But the damned get high to find perfect repose
> And a wine-bottle lies in the corner of a cloud.
> So many tragedies have gone down time unnoticed like
> breathing
> . . .
> I'll swing in my life, my death, the way that I want to.

The freewheeling figure of Postell drawn by these contemporaries is more complicated, however. Joans' statement that "Black poets read *to* Beatniks" is his not-so-gentle reminder of the cooperating but segregated literary communities a Black poet like Postell was forced to negotiate. Kean's poem, on the other hand, addresses issues of autonomy and damnation always on the table for such a poet in the process. Any notion of "crossing between" escalates further when reading Kean's 1961 poem against the national backdrop of Freedom Riders, Robert Williams, and the Tougaloo Nine. The "swinging in my life, my death" here thus plays doubletime: resonating both with a basic need to *live*, to breathe, and to occupy earthly space—and the always having to physically and spiritually fight for it.

Incidentally, Kean guides us into a central ambition of Postell's work, one that feels palpably political: *wishing*. One of Tom's most anthologized poems continues to be "I Want a Solid Piece of Sunlight," not merely because it has been one of the three or four poems Tom has left editors up to now. It's a certified banger, literally an "underground" anthem for those wishing for worldly space:

> Let us enter the redundant oasis which rips of
> jungle beats on glasses of gin.
> We never get on the train that stops to let the
> morning messenger in.
> And with rats digging in the cellar the basement
> cement crumbles as we rise.
> Lakes of icy whispering trees float crunchingly on
> under the glory of wide blue sky:
> O give me a solid piece of sunlight and a yardstick
> of my own and the right to holler.

Postell's need to holler freely is a common impulse in much of *Tomb*, often taking the form of a "wild wishing" romantic gesture. Frequently poems are portraits of beloveds or addresses to them and, as in "Sunlight" above, Postell enlists any material he can into his wishing that its outcome might prove successful. Spaces and places are carved, natural images are conjured like messengers, and the imagination is given license to compose an order according to what it sees as ideal harmony. "Sandra," "Model at Her Mirror," "Poem [butterflies]," and "The Girl in the Garden" (a poem whose muse could arguably be a young Rona Jaffe) are stunning examples of Postell wishing his words into something as durably "ultra real" as his vast emotional interior. Trees become "Turning green world, rollicking in grief, round aspirin of love" and loud city nights portend "[his] day's dolphin drifting thru the west." This kind of astonishing imagery is often curated by an interlocutor or speaker who sums these parts to existential sense—into a kind of refrain or dominant melodic theme.

Even when poems aren't using overt song structure, this sonic carving lends them a potent *sense* of song—often a blues reminiscent of Langston Hughes, or to go back further, the rhapsodic Raymond Garfield Dandridge, one of his Cincinnati forebears (Price Hill, to be exact). Postell's desire to fashion his poems as acoustic space extends to his use of typographic materials. Idiosyncrasy of stanza break, indentation, and punctuation abound in *Tomb*-era poems, peaking in the untitled "[There they sit vacantly     the]":

There they sit vacantly     the

star,ing at the cards     light

until night calls them     is

with his tow,ering might     strong

to sleep.     on


There they s,it at breakfast     me

star,ing at the morning news     who

un,til., they must work                              am

until a certain time later                                    I

th,ey stare at m,e I                        who

am being stared at and it                        are

is st,range.                                                        you

                                                    ?

A unidentifiable social exchange—between patrons in a diner or coffeeshop—becomes an absurdist play of surveillance and countersurveillance, complete with interrogation. The poem is full of literal staring and glancing, but recruits commas and other divided visual structures to give it a glancing rhythm as well. The experience of reading it is fantastical as a result: somehow its run of notes feels both instantaneous and elongated. Personhood and purpose are stretched to the maximum. The poem is not unlike a mid-1960's Eric Dolphy tune: patched together horn blips and squeals that atomize a moment into something vast, interstellar.

By the mid-1960's, Postell's shape is dithering in Baraka's autobiography: as Baraka moves toward a different portion of the stage, the fresnel light on Postell fades. There's tenderness in Baraka's portraiture of Postell—an intimacy and a sadness in what one can only read as a quickly atomizing friendship. You can hear: *We were tight.* Composed some fifteen years prior to Postell's actual death, "For Tom Postell, Dead Black Poet," thus reads more as an elegy for camaraderie and its shared (or diverging) ideologies. Little is known about Tom's New York City day-to-day during these years, but evidence suggests that he faced adversity by the middle of the decade.

In the early through mid-sixties, Manhattan saw an uptick in deadly drinking parties it hadn't seen since the fifties, fueled by cheap illegally bottled alcohol cut with methyl spirits. According to sister Katherine and wife Rose Bianchi, Tom attended such a party at some point in the mid-sixties and, along with a number of attendees, was taken into Bellevue for treatment and observation. The lasting effects were severe enough that his stay was prolonged, giving an unscrupulous landlord cause to evict him and trash most of his possessions. Itinerancy followed, with Tom floating between friends' places, weekly hotels, and presumably, men's missions. Fearing her brother's death by exposure, his youngest sister Pauline phoned Katherine who lived in New Jersey, and they arranged to bring him back to Cincinnati.

It's challenging to assign Postell to any single ecosystem of Black poetics within the ever-changing artistic landscape between 1950 and 1970 (and I'd posit that it's counterproductive to delimit him too much here). Within the confines of a brief introduction, it's a hazard to attempt thorough explication of the literary and political movements he was likely in conversation with—the Beats, Black Mountain Poets, Black Arts, Umbra, New York School, Black Power (either Revolutionary or Cultural Nationalism), and the Nation of Islam. He swims in much of it. Aligning Tom with jazz aesthetics is a whole other conversation. Is he swing or is he bop? Hard-bop or modal free? Tom's reading and listening habits were varied but he played favorites: Cecil Taylor, Miles, T.S. Eliot, Don Lee, Ornette Coleman, Aimé Césaire, Charles Mingus, Ezra Pound, Sarah Vaughn, Rimbaud, Eric Dolphy, Carolyn Rodgers, James Joyce. There's likely an entire essay to be plumbed on the aesthetic and biographical synchrony of Postell with his hero Mingus: as Rose Bianchi relates, Mingus' death in 1979 caused Postell to leave his postal job early, inconsolably in tears.

Up to his death in 1980, his repertoire remains an amalgam of influences, compulsions, and preferences. Like a musician, he has standards. The spleen of his work seems always to be fin-de-siecle French—the grimy yet luminous surrealism of Rimbaud and the decadent, cursed visions of Verlaine. My co-editor Anthony Sutton does remarkable work in this volume to survey this trail of French Romanticism in Postell's style, with particular attention to his quest for a new Black vernacular that is magical by virtue of its deviance from "permissible" or "predictable" kinds of readability. We must follow this question into another: how did Tom's work holler in crowded concert with that of his similarly subversive peers? While most poems of *The Tomb* predate the founding of the Black Arts Repertory Theater and School (BARTS) in 1965 and the assassination of Malcom X (two of movement's alpha points), his work nonetheless shares ethical and ontological questions central to Black Arts and Black Power. As Etheridge Knight asserts in a landmark 1968 issue of *Negro Digest*:

> Unless the Black artist establishes a "Black aesthetic" he will have no future at all. To accept the white aesthetic is to accept and validate a society that will not allow him to live. The Black artist must create new forms and new values, sing new songs (or purify old ones); and along with other Black authorities, he must create a new history, new symbols, myths, and legends (and purify old ones by fire). And the Black artist, in creating his own aesthetic, must be accountable for it only to the Black people. Further, he must hasten his own dissolution as an individual (in the Western sense)—painful though the process may be, having been breast-fed the poison of "individual experience."

# *GERTRUDE STEIN* RIDES THE TOWN DOWN EL
## - to New York City

Then colors rose through the leaves in light
        surprise.
The last peacock poised and sighed on the leaves
        and rose.
Wonderful day careens while blighted riff-raff
        children skate and
Laughingly dig the hole for the mid-western
        bonfire.
Wrap honey in velvet air and hide it in October's
        searching breath.
The bonfire dwindles as the circus leaves and
        the animals roar.
It's only in the sun that madness splatters into
        joy . . .
Cover down the moon for the night before you
        lift the skirts of a cloud.
Love knocks on the inside of my skull and kicks
        in my stomach.
A doe licks the gum from a tree and runs into
        the woods.
She lets me govern her gaze when the parade
        blares its colors.
Gertrude Stein is long dead but under cover rides
        the torn down El.

Postell's self-corrected contributor copy of Yugen No. 1 (1958).
Courtesy of Rose Bianchi.

The aesthetic and the ethical must regain alignment for liberatory process to occur. Poems, as Baraka famously writes in "Black Art," must be "like fists . . . Assassin poems. Poems that shoot / guns." Postell is no stranger to direct political discourse in *Tomb* and especially in his later drafts and journaling. Poems like "Jamboree," "They Shot J.F.K.," "Dancing on Stone," "Video," and "Poem [boy]" are deeply committed to the same new ideological embodiment—a Blackness becoming and becoming fluently Black—as burgeoning Black Power. However, the oft-cited fists and guns of "Black Art" often eclipse the same poem's opening proviso that "Poems are bullshit unless they are / teeth or trees or lemons piled / on a step." Ultra-real, yes, but not immune to the imagination's appetite for arrangement and improvisation. Postell's poetry revels in imagistic and linguistic arrangements that become fluent in themselves, like a personal iconography or the "new myth" that Knight sees as necessary for nation-building. The unfurling banner of "Even If" is a prime example of Postell associatively building at fever-pitch:

> No. No. Don't form dark clouds in my sky this day.
> Nor this night when sleek lanes lead to the moon's lambent glades.
> Where drunken Gods whittle seriousness into willows falling to their knees,
> their trembling knees that rock the mud and foam
> until daylight shakes with laughter laughing and then wanes when
> love parks among these shadows seducing white lightning . . .
> This vague blues floats over a bridge with sorrowful foundations.
> Our knees are trembling holding up the vibrating mountain
> while angels dance through these dreams whispering love words
> among the crumbling sands trickling through the hands of the meadow clocks.

Like another of his great heroes, Charlie Parker, Postell aims for unrelenting inventiveness of phrase and image. And like Parker—who also happened to be a skilled drummer—Postell wants to expand his voice rhythmically across space-time: from pentameter ("their trembling knees . . .") to a modified 3-beat swing ("among the crumbling . . .) complete with a stressed turnaround ("clocks"). Marvelously rich with reference and resonance, the poem conjures a complete universe in the face of cosmic deterioration. Amoeba-like language moves to fill the negative space of an often-punishing reality, and long lines give the self some stay against entropy. Rent's always due, the train uptown takes forever, and the beloved gets jaded. There's gritty heroism to Tee's "vague blues," just as there is to the musical medium: the blues will always, as Albert Murray writes, "modify the form to meet the exigencies of the situation." Suddenly, we're not that far off from surrealism at its most political. The artist brings their whole arsenal of materials to bear not just on the material problem of daily living, but the problem of being behind it.

Like improvised solos gyring around melodic centers, many of Tom's poems actively suspend time (and selfhood) in this way. In "the painful memory and the waylaid hope," the speaker tries to glean selfhood in the existential equation. Tom opts for short, curtailed lines that make us wait for each new piece of the algebra. It's a quick step, almost militant:

> and who can deny time
> is movement
> and waits at both ends
> its own end
> and the reason for pain
> in movement is pain
> holds the event of suicide

balanced on the scales
with life
in strained relationships
among nations
and one is the answer
or zero is the answer
—as either of the two
approach the world
it approaches me
who am the painful memory
and the waylaid hope
waiting for the world
to make one or nothing

Postell's waywardness might be more tangible as a *waylaidness* in this regard, a subversiveness that also feels vulnerable. If a dream deferred might explode, as Langston Hughes hypothesizes, one *composing* of that explosion might very well take the form of a Postell poem. It's work that builds habitable space at the interstice of futility and futurity, the practical and the visionary. The many ways Postell can *produce* this space—his willingness to remain off-center, "crucial and alone" as Audre Lorde writes—is what makes him capable of such profound and astonishing intimacy. One of the great challenges of this volume has been to typeset Tom's poems according to the space they claim for themselves. When Postell goes photonic and long across the page, capturing this poetic space-time is a feat and an obligation. It's in Tom's entension that we feel most his reaching for himself, and for us. We've endeavored to give Postell's lines all the domain they ask.

Postell's final decade in Cincinnati brought him back into fellowship with both music and poetry to a degree. Afternoons were spent at colleague Donald "Snooky" Gibson's barbershop on Reading at Union in Avondale—what elders tell me they still call "The Cincinnati Cultural and Intellectual Center." Snooky's sat just around the corner from the site of the long-gone Babe Baker's, stopover for Coltrane, Johnny Griffin, and Sonny Stitt. The barbershop existed twice due to bulging university development and another interstate corridor. Rahsaan Roland Kirk, one old session lion tells me, pioneered his double-horn technique at Babe's before moving on to three. Intersections, like the genetic code of Cincinnati.

He spent evenings with wife Rose, cooking dinner, listening to records, and typing. He continued to make work, though less regularly, and always hunting the same speed and space in *Seasons* he'd achieved in Manhattan. Surrealism, once the *de rigeur* of innovation, had become anachronism by the 1970's. We catch Postell's later work (selections of which we've included here) mid-metamorphoses and toward a different martial tune—worthy of an entire introduction in itself. We find him nonetheless pursuing these "words without pages, songs without spaces," a fearless wild wishing that might become one or nothing.

A perfect rimshot occurs when a drummer's stick strikes the drumskin and its frame simultaneously. The crack produced is a moment of supreme unity—between what is rigid and what might break. The stick will splinter with enough force. A drummer can achieve the most resonance by striking the snare just *off*-center. This, we'd submit, is perfectly Postell and in his spirit, we hope this volume hits right there.

Postell in a suit sewn for him by Rose,
Cincinnati, Christmas 1975, Photo courtesy of Rose Bianchi.

POEMS

from *Poems from the Tomb*
(1953–1969)

# The Tomb

A shadow shocked in morphine
Glowering behind a bongo drum
Cries out in the colored smoke
    And what sorcery drives that other shade's
    Hands over that vibraphone
    Playing with smirking secrets
Over hollow holes of intermittence

Now someone plays a wrong note
One soul drowns in a big sea
As the ping ping saves my soul
Held dangling by its navel string
From the changing of the key

        They are watching me
Who am mummy of love chaste in window

# Charlie Parker Died

The moon struck dumb
was high and wailing
soaking in a sodden
great black heart. Aloft thru
the quiet drone of
the Hero's dream: it was adrift among stars and blackness.

Billie Holiday stood before the door of his tomb
chained to it singing the blues.
He climbed onto the rooftop among stars drifting light
and drove his sounds thru the black burning sky.

He swung above the sea of love below
and thru long sad days blowed the banner of sunken dreams.
And the seablooms, and the seawinds, threaded
flooding tubes through sunken shadows, through patterns
on the sea's floor scorning and swooping the surface with a
storm of architectural sound from
bloom roots that shot and burst plainer forms of communication
than can be tooted by silly demons huddling
over mountains of oversimplifications
reorganizing this sordid plan that spring has.

He told them to close the door that
wild flowers open softly singing, and
starve that heart of sunlight and levity
and let Him eat doom.

               He eschewed it and
consumed that void. And sadness was torn and beaten

for wearing baggy pants to church, and from womb to
womb. Wind this story on spools of agony, O lovely Lord.
Agony of soul. Elephants laugh at pity piled high
as the giant shit hills of hell. During the resurrection
he took the barbed wire from the Lord and laid down the law.
Our pretenses and beliefs were lies and dead.
He cried
because He cried. Big teardrops fell thru the moonshine
onto barren earth. Renunciation of
green shoots blew bright sunbulbs that splattered
pinkeyed whirlwinds through jazz songs minstrels introduced
to last lotus squatting buffaloes.

## The Deuce

a cigarette falls lightly to the floor
the crowd hums
dim stars giggle
outside this wooden building
which shakes with the
rhythm of the jazz band
and now is not now
but parallel to yesterday
since we are that far away from ourselves

a humming bird
blows the saxophone
propped on the wine glass rim
soft wine waves
lap the sides of the glass
and the air is smoke
around this world

good or bad
nothing is more
than smoke now

the possum preaches from his rostrum
hat in hand and mind in jar
flashing diamond eyes . . .

I am drowsy
here
where the clock has its absolute tick
: a tick tocks a tick

## I Want a Solid Piece of Sunlight and a Yardstick to Measure It With

Seventh Avenue fills at noon with a gray tide of
      suits come out for air.
Noon catching fire peeks over the high rooftops
      and spits into the saloons.
The brown buildings drip with wilting plaster and
      the mighty pigeon's dung.
Sylphindine Fifth Avenue trips on red and green
      lights and slides quietly by Central Park.
Honeysuckle leaps over the hedges as the people
      leave Staten Island for work.
Long Island slides in its channel groaning under
      the new load of grinding storms.
I see the Brooklyn Dodgers on Times Square with
      their bats and balls practicing.
Let us enter the redundant oasis which rips of
      jungle beats on glasses of gin.
We never get on the train that stops to let the
      morning messenger in.
And with rats digging in the cellar the basement
      cement crumbles as we rise.
Lakes of icy whispering trees float crunchingly on
      under the glory of wide blue sky:
O give me a solid piece of sunlight and a yardstick
      of my own and the right to holler.
I don't need to ask for the moon cause I love some-
      thing that melts in your breath.

# Zoom Home

Mailor cut his wife
I cut myself while shaving and
My girl cut her teeth
Bursting my balloon stored many ages of this ageless
Society as assorted candy beloved clandestinity
Zooooooooooms home.

A man wants to be Henry Miller but is afraid
To give up his dollars and his insanity, combs
His hair in our elevator cause he says we are
Swine like him. His hillbillies and our hillbillies
Have much in common. O Ethiopiana!
These snapshots took their time to tow my God
While many feet trickled thru love's lips
And lines drove along whispering these things hither
Thither thru old time and new beloved clandestinity
Zooooooooooms home.

## Poem

I countered and crashed
And smashed
The fish bowl broke
And I jumped up and ran

A dancing sea horse . . .
Maybe he's crazy

I countered and crashed
And broke
Spread all over truth
And I jumped back and ran

Small children are happy
At Xmastime

I got up and ran
And kissed her sweating thighs
The left one     The right one

Fish get away from it all

I countered and crashed
The mirror was a window pane

# They Shot J.F.K.

Not only for that day and the ones that follow do we
Hunt the lost words and build sanitariums for our hearts
But for the preceding hours that built the catastrophe too tall
When God made us smaller than our smoking souls reaching high
Through the air as hate rises from passionate throats of love.

Nor for filled paper of empty words to please the mourners
Do we long while the sun is filling the world attic with shadows or
Whimper after the moon when J.F.K. lies buried like a root in the ground
While we are lost on the desert overloaded with a useless oasis filled with
J.F.K.'s blood endlessly toiling thru our hearts for no good reason
Thrilling the audience color drunk and trying to get their feet out of mud.

We like the audience struggle and reach frantically for non-blooms
Among fire blowing up love's bubble in America's washing machine.

## Moon Rocks for Mother

I chopped moon rocks, with
the stump ends on old ink pens, I found
discarded by old golf greats on old green country clubs, they built
on the floating islands they tried to dam the river with, O
I dug a hole to drop the rocks, and posed, rocks in hands, dropping them,
divorcing them, one by one, like I did the nineteenth century French poets,
    freeing them, dropping them

through swollen throats, of birds splashing up from hell, I told them
the hole was too much like a pussy, the rocks too real, falling like the
    shadow of Christ, on our loved ones, I

twisted the springs of my clock so tight they can never move again, I drove
my shoulders and my ass through the leaden clock works, she
told me Paris was love and New York money, I was hung upside down on a
    weeping willow, and I scampered after her with it swishing like a tail.

I drank great wines and dialed long distance operators all over the world.
I told them I am a black man and I just zipped down the seams of my soul.
I hung up before they could answer, except for Copenhagen, I
heard no answer from Copenhagen: they said Kierkegaard was dead now.
For long days, I sat with tongue in cheek watching television, watching laughter.

Climbing from the hole in the ground I dropped all my rocks.
They fell with disdain
and struck bland brains then sang, the mad
woman I met burning old gossip columns buttoned my shirt, I
told her that the sea was to blame.

And she believed me.

Plop.

# For . . .

*—to James Henue*

Have you ever written down a night
as a phantom white face breaks through?
So I turn to kiss the palm of her hand—
they don't believe in love here—the building crumbles.

She won't sit still, watch her get up and sing.
The night like her hair hovers around her face.
She sings of the Star of David and hope
and when she has retreated through her veil of space
she shoots firearms because that is what the world has given her.

It is better that I, the Black Phantom, remain estranged
from this bulge world, this fantastic bulge of idiot brains.

Our wings disperse stars as silly as afternoons.
Why does she shrink from her joy of smiling?
I sum it up by applying to her a dream:

I saw God picking pretty things from a rose bush
and sang and danced among its thorns.

# The Metamorphosis of Black Ophelia

Black Ophelia      Black Ophelia
Won't you ever understand the coursing
Of my blood through channels of yourself?

Black Ophelia      Black Ophelia
Let me look into your glass black eyes that glare
With the fury of the Atlantic Ocean and surround
Me and drown me until I am drunk on my gasping breath and
Gladly sink down to blissfully totter on the floor of the sea.

Dry, mercenary Ophelia your sun has gone down
Behind white clouds of gathering tears that wait for that
Calamitous day when the umbrella will not be good enough
To ward off the arrows of the rising sea
Where I am, where I, where I am waiting for you.

Black      Black Ophelia when you then sink down
To the mouth of the sea
I'll find you and wrap you in weed
And secure you to a turtle's back
Who'll swim forever near the water's surface
Where you will burn darker in the hot sunlight
And glow like a sapphire in the pale moonlight
And giggle when that final calamitous rain comes
Filling the universe with my eyes.

## Charlie Parker in Bohemia

too nonchalant to terrify us
—presidents trying to prove themselves common place
sneak off into the night when the security forces are sleeping
and drive recklessly over the backroads of New England towns
the souped up automobiles of our desire

we owls watch quietly and fill up our bags
with these secrets and wait patiently til we are overburdened
and then we move through the sky like gentlemen
when day has foreclosed on Charlie Parker in Bohemia

# The Girl in the Garden

*—For Rona*

A box of light on small round wheels
Rollicked through a silk black tube
Emerged into the bright sunlight
Erupting me on sandpaper concrete
To crawl into the Garden of Eden.

And there was dancing a pale-faced girl
More beautiful than Mitchell's silver thought
Who sprayed me with peppermint life
—her big eyes swelled in the smile of mind
In this Garden of Eden.

She was tuned with stereophonic sound
Vibrating through her body and out her mouth
Were words like fruits falling off tall trees
Playing down through the watery air
Into the Garden of Eden.

Clouds of glowing crowds watch shining
Like snowing tinsel on Christmas trees
In the birth drunk Sunday light
In this Garden of Eden.

And I stood up and danced, too, on the cushion grass
Catching the fruits as they fell from the trees
And the box of light rolled back into the silk black tube
From the Garden of Eden.

# Ann

As firm air presents
gently scented words from her mouth
the light stings her yellow hair
—haloes a natural Shelley stare.

From those eyes hot light pours out
beams of formidable gentility,
unwavering projection,
mad languid interception.

Facing this smiling apparition
scent of licorice on her lips
and small bubble breasts
I sigh. She is jaded.
The moment hangs. She is faded.

Shelley's soul is flashing red,
he poses on the bed.
She shuffles on the wooden floor
and hurries barefoot out the door.

She flees through this petrified putrefaction
as Shelley and I turn to stone.

## [There they sit vacantly     the]

There they sit vacantly     the

star,ing at the cards     light

until night calls them     is

with his tow,ering might     strong

to sleep.     on


There they s,it at breakfast     me

star,ing at the morning news     who

un,til.,! they must work     am

until a certain time later     I

th,ey stare at m,e I     who

am being stared at and it     are

is st,range.     you

     ?

## Poem

I.
Succeed the game of love
Rise above the shores of Galilee
Platoon your sighs for one alone
Condone the shortest kiss
But never miss
Life alone is hard as stone.

Tranquil the pulsing of your veins
Decide when your heart shall beat faster
Dethrone disaster
of two breaking arms of desire
Walk into her house and ask her
for some fire
God will hold your reins.

Verbs shall be your angels
Withhold their source
Turn her to the sun and tell her
of your remorse
And sad in the beginning
Rise above the shores of Galilee
to the source

Of life unwinding
intertwining
in her heart's spangles.

She so sad sometimes as she is happy
Deserves words drawn by elegant churchmen
Wildmen of belief, chargers that pilfer night

—Game bird of her desire, rise into her hair
And make a pillow warm on winter's frozen chair.

II.
Nocturnal moon
Nonchalant loon
Rolling through this gloomy room
Insurrectionist of doom
Make our arms bloom

III.
Love like my love roam
And find suction,
Kill destruction,
Defeat obstruction, lay
down our silent dome
So we can burst through it
Like an erection-silent
metamorphoses of the crucifixion.

IV.
Steeple bell do climb
In bellowing chime
I am going to an inspection
Of my soul.

V.
Love is afflicted by the landlord's rent:
Gold lines my love's way;
My whole life is spent;
When she is gone away.

# I Have No Domain, I Have No Moon

When one must find a home:
Nature holds on to her finicky chains,
the heart has only a breast to beat in:
Love builds a waterfall on an enchanted planet.

I waited for the afternoon express.
It seems it got lost in the desert dust.
I boarded the midnight train for Zanzibar.
I arrived home at half past two.
Half-hearted and full of tears as a defunct waterfall.

A lantern built
to burn light to blue and joy
grew from two eyes that sang sad
songs, that roamed the glades of Fifth Avenue.

When one must find a home:
Dreams denounce their princely prerogatives,
the soul sands down its own statue made of stone:
Love entangles itself in a network wrought of thorns.

A town was raised
among us
like a being deftly human,
—a town of pretenses and absolutes,
and eyes were raised above this stage,
bright odes urging love to prepare.

All over the world simple souls raise up their arms.
Firemen, eternally asleep, rush out and pull down these
    false alarms.

When one must find a home:
Nature and dreams dance to a jolly tune,
the spirit sits upon its lofty throne and laughs:
Love redoubles its strength and lays down the law;
When one must find a home.

Bright conning morning.
How much rent will you try to collect?
I have no moon, no love, I have no domain.
I boarded the midnight train for Zanzibar
because I thought I would find love there.
Instead there began my sojourning.

A culture turned inside her soul.
A clown reined on a pedestal in her heart.
A jack-o-lantern led her crusades.
She rode with the statue of the park
Into the sun going down, and after dark
I tore down the milky way, and
tried to resurrect her in the sky.

I went from Spain to Japan to the North Pole.
I bought a round trip ticket on the midnight express.
I found myself buried in the desert dust.
I bailed out of the plane over Zanzibar.
I arrived home at half past two.
I found love, umbrella open, hiding behind the Metropolitan
    Opera House.

All over the world simple souls raise up their arms.
Firewomen, eternally asleep, rush out and pull down
    these false alarms.

O lantern moon! reap our departures! sing
solidarity! O lantern moon! turn us loose!

## Poem

I would like to write a poem
more beautiful than a tree
about my friends that make it in the art world
and about the art world too
flowers for them
stems for their arms
and roots to the mothers
squares and druthers
moons and winds
sounds that tell the truth
people that give up their virginity to a rolling stone
squares and druthers
and shit

I would like to write a poem
more beautiful than a tree
and sell it to a dog

## The Young Know the Old Are Dead

Whip who
to what shit
better start to run
to stop
ending
on a hang up.

Whip which
sprung
ideas
I told a long time ago

ending
on a hang up.

Whip who?

Sprung ideas.

To start
and to stop
them.

Lousy Lou
sprung those ideas
I told a long time ago.

I'll never tell them again.

Whip who

into what great shit?
The young know the
old are dead
and time has kicked itself in the ass.

This noise blinds
blinds itself
and the wind takes away the ashes.

## Poem

If no bugs come out of the typewriter
If nothing steals the moment
If there is no love and the evening ends
My time
My choice
My ridiculous sense of love
If nothing redeems itself
My little black girl
Humble star of thunder escapes my hands
My little black girl
Mine
Release and gather the running seam of my mother's stocking

To tell the truth
Repeatedly requires a sense of the lie
My whole life is a lie
When I wrote of love
When I said I loved
When those that love stood up and cheered
that was all a lie
My little black girl
Do you remember
When we wrote our love on the wall
So afraid to tell each other
They took us to the kiss
And we fought to keep away from what we wanted
My little black girl
Do you remember

## [Amoeboid]

Amoeboid
Breathing in mud, strangling on salt
My eyes glare
I am blind
A bee buzzes beside me
The wind blows
The sun drops its heat
While I wait for the dust
To saturate me
Up from hell or down from heaven
An exposed exterior
Sits on my spreaded splotch
Pompously laughing.
The rhythm patter patter
Clatters for my brain.
On the tongue of ocean
Stuttering jazz
Splashing in the wash
Detritus from my feet
I see the jewels
That hung around the soul of fish
I see the jewels that hung around the soul of fish
Rising up to greet me with insurmountable inspiration
Like a fart on an elevator
The glitter of gold laid inlaid in rubies in a chest
Hidden in a cavern
I am nevermore
Now in the interjectory
As we go foolishly and slow
Through the intermittent tunnel
A forging funnel

Leaving a thin trail of dung.
This I is that that
The that that is
The train is this that I am

Choo        chooooo        chooooooo        choooooooooo

Through the mirage
        Through the image
                Through the mirror

Choooooooo        choooooooooo        choooooooooooooooooooo

    Through it all at once
Forever.

# The Rabbit Was Rimbaud

A rabbit ran after his tail
until the rhythm in his back set sail
in the wind-blown sea of grass.

When far away from feather feet
he thought of the green of old home
where the shelter of yellow carrots
in the sun dripped the dew
into the oblique eyes of the fairy

of the sad field of love.

He ran after his tail
until his hop became a bouncing shadow
out of which his eyes went around
as burning balls of carrots.

The rabbit was Rimbaud
dancing the carrots.

## An Accordion of Love

Plato held up my blood red heart
to shine into the big eyes of love
and it became a lamp of hope.

I looked back
to see one girl
in the red glow of my heart.

Plato and my bulging eyes made me so drunk
and sick I vomited my lungs and their words
and was nearly strangled by the veins.

I lay a mess on a city street
with my bulging eyeballs
reaching to see who she was
as rising up in me my intestines
gargled out my mouth
pulling on my whirling squares
pulling me in like an accordion
—I called a name I thought was hers.

Letting out again
and in
and out
I rang silver sounds in my brains.
She was my lamp of hope
while I lay a mess on a city street.

I bent my lips and called another name
belched the stuff

pulled in again
oozed out slimy words of love.

No response: she was numb.
I reached my hand
into the pocket
pulled the wine
and drank
and laughed

belched the stuff again

oozed out slimy words of love:

I became an accordion of love
playing to a lone deaf street lamp.

TOM POSTELL

## Poem

A billboard of desire and a cobweb of torn sky destroyed a subway train
moving through the air . . .

Unknown to all the lights that play along the sky when God disturbs them
pretending to be sad and lonely I am lost along Broadway.

Poets climb the hurting noonday hurrying masses like James Henue naked
carrying in a little Kiddie Kart a distraught typewriter.

Oh there are so many beautiful things that I have seen and do now wish
to see again and again.

Lord help us love the preciosity of the image well-done and spread like
a feast for us old human beings when we wake up.

Now I thrive and when I do not thrive I thrust home with another's line
if I can remember it tomorrow.

THE UNSUNG MASTERS SERIES

Will not this end and when I do unto this and that changing and exchanging
and refusing wills from sex-happy old bitches that don't know
it is their only kindness.

And making mistakes.

Lord of love grant me any wish that can be returned to you.

Flowers can remove their own wild glory when they fade into spring
and turn out their little petals to fan the air and my love's
eyelashes blink at me.

Cars move unloved and will continue doing so until . . .

69

# Poem

A man from Japan
rode a horse through the gorge
    to the borders of the blue sea
onward through the borders of the sea
forward through the sea sagebrush
hair blown back by the drifting currents
he rode his big bay stud through the seaweed
to ownership and untaxed existence among the laughing sea life.

A man from Japan
rode an intercontinental ballistic missile
from the castles of Tokyo to the arid plateaus in Utah
upon the arid planes of my uncensored mind
to find me crosslegged on the stone
before an ivory image of an angel
I had carved into the left tusk of elephant
who stands on his right tusk smirking
while I exhort, I exhort the angel
    to kiss me then
I will dedicate my first book of poems to her.

The man from Japan
rode the horse through the gorge
    to the borders of the blue sea
onward through the borders of the sea
forward through the sea sagebrush
hair blown back by the drifting currents
he rode his big bay stud through the seaweed
to ownership and untaxed existence among the laughing sea life.

# Could Her Sin Have Been Good Sin

She stands before the altar
golden brown and full of sorrow
could her sin have been good sin
she would not be here
in the barn
in the ice-house
when all the world is ready to fight.

Could her sin have been good sin
she would not be here
when I have entered looking
for her, for her who received my heart
in her hands and threw it away
and ran away to Holland looking
for free admission to a church
of God.

Could her sin have been good sin
she would not be here
lost on her knees like a beggar
and growing in my mind among
the steeples and the candles rising up
into this vast emptiness which
is my heart because it has no
direction.

She left only a building under construction
girders mortar planks, and sweating flesh
on eyes crying
the clarity of the moon
an open mouth

about to speak
words it never heard
and a soul about to gather up its belongings
walk up to the altar of the Mother Mary
and inquire of her the reason
behind its birth.

Could her sin have been good sin
she would not be here
and neither would I.

## Poem

Boom, gone doom, run room, of my love, the safety catch won't loosen dear.
Pretend to cream, baby, loan me, the afternoon shudders, and duck your head, boom.
Mistress, undress, redress in courts, and bloom in the drawers, while Lila laughs:
Do unto others as others do unto themselves. Don't look at me that way, I am shy.

Why do we motor to the beginning to pronounce our end, then opening our traps, cry?
Believe in moving vans and a bird's heart on fire when you love, dream.
Close to the start, and forgiven the end, love is the running goose that stops to speak.
Don't ever pretend to hate, hate, how are we born, but love, win the prize, flow.
Descend, begin with me to sing. Let's uncork the bottle and drink the blood, halt.
I am tired of writing poems. I want to lie in her arms and go to sleep. Goodbye.

# Jamboree

*For from this instant,*
*There's nothing serious in mortality:*
*All is but toys: renown and grace is dead*
                    *—Macbeth, II:iii*

Jamboree:
The silent heart waits
for sorcery. The dictator raises the baton
and the bartenders clap in glee.

Jamboree:
The scent of pink poodle dogs on the make
is sorcery. The silent heart waits
to ring a bell out over the sea. Serious birds
mount the air like it is a silent staircase of laughter.

Jamboree:
People reach into their heads
pull out the silver strings of memory
and tie them around their tongues
and are afraid to speak again,
even in this jamboree.

# the painful memory and the waylaid hope

all our sorrow grew the heavy cloud
which has taken over the sky
where the rainbow waits at its own end
ominously warning what it will take
for them to switch places

in the sky or the heart
a cloud of smoke
or thoughts that choke
both waylay hope
smothering it
regardless of the imminence of time
and who can see the next minute
if the one present is thick enough
to fill and pacify two wet eyes
and why be thin
when the danger of thinness is transparency
or death
. . . thick or thin death
and who can deny time
is movement
and waits at both ends
its own end
and the reason for pain
in movement is pain
holds the event of suicide
balanced on the scales
with life
in strained relationships
among nations
and one is the answer

or zero is the answer
—as either of the two
approach the world
it approaches me
who am the painful memory
and the waylaid hope
waiting for the world
to make one or nothing

## Delores

She is the black of an eclipsed moon
When Christ hung on his cross
The purist bastard, my foster father
Alone in the night, aloft in herself
She becomes my invisible angel
Withholding from me my destiny
Whispering out of nothingness a song
A song in the nightsound wind
She stands aloft in herself a lighthouse
For which I am a ship riding a tidal wave
With no will for direction being led
Pulled towards eternity by love:
The lighthouse stands aloft on the sea
I careen maddened by the murky waves

## Poem

Death done
I have won
and lay down the spade
for the light that hides in shade
overcome by honor
I call out to her
and hearing no return
I scorn my urn
and lap the sides of that ship

O I lap the sides of that ship
that sailed and made her eyes drip

She left only ignorance
an illegal desire
a child's stance
for hire
I awoke and roamed the world for rest
my hands helped my broken legs as best
they could

I stride unaware
all I love and care for doesn't care
I want to tear the muscles from the sea
and leave them bare, but I don't dare—
they might strangle you and me

## Tomorrow

in the dust of yesterday
today is today, and towards
evening, love is tear juice
                    in lemonade

from winter to summer
        spring comes to fire

bursting and; bursting

friendly sex
in the evening of tomorrow
towards the destination

we will sit
she will knit a bit
we will sit
she will cry a bit
we will sit
I will sigh a bit
        in the evening
        of tomorrow
                    towards our destination

# Poem

How it rains! She sticks a pin into my gloom. It bursts.
A whole ocean turns to steam. Out of the steam a girl tip-toes.
The legions of whip-bearing bosses stand naked growling.
We run. I run from her. She runs from the steam. Our tears run. I hate.
Rain falls. O love! Where is your resting place? When you turn the flicker glows.

The heat burns our bare hearts black. It's up to her. Take her steam bath.
The heavy doors slam into my face. I can't see with these flattened eyes.
I can hear her breathing. Rain. Oppression. I love beauty; but I am afraid.
Her eyes melt into rain drops in the blue night and fall through the moonlight.
Wet. I am wet. I don't care. When the rain falls I am washed til I am beautiful.

## Poem

voice of void girl jams the concert tubes of thought.
air turns back into the room and breathes autumn, doldrums.
girl smiles or doesn't smile, she wanders idly by.
love has ridden astray on an eagle's back, happiness clings to a memory, one thinks
in the evening after a ringing hell-bell day, lights drown the room, sighing.
how beautiful can love and girl be? when does the line draw itself.
she wanders by, old dead flowers droop sadly, the afternoon is doldrums.
I am glad she is happy and I hope she gets happier, I hope she gets happier.
. . . pain of life without her, no form of love, did she ever really care, really?
poets get pity, poets sit on shady river banks, life moves only for the fortunate.
well swept rugs, blooms of going-to die roses, girls are God, I worship.
friendship, after girls lets be friends, flowering afternoon, cream.
songs of buildings, roofs of pigeons, gently pushing winds, sing-song night.
of all the girls in the world she did not even look at me, run reason, climb arrogance, powder.
afternoon of her eyes, autumn hair roan rumbling down, the wind in her skirt, she dreams.
streetcars and her feet move as the light changes, she returns into the smoke. I . . .
because of morning I remember that clouds descend, the blue sky never ends.
return to her island eyes and hide, sing bouquets of memories, begin to believe.
—it's not night, day tips to the starting line and prays, bang, bang, love.

## Poem

Lila is.
    Silvery tick tocks
    Night sprawls on afternoon.
Lila is.
    Ophelia blows up balloons of wistfulness.
I awoke one morning in her eyes crying.
Lila is.
    Poet's hearts beat like drums in a parade.
Her feet press lightly on the concrete when she walks.
Her voice sounds like a trumpet made of silk when she talks.
Lila.
Burn this.
Gargle with its juice.
I stand in the window.
I look over the rooftops for you.
Morning hooks and reels in night
as I reach out for you.
And blending, falling into you
I disentangle my little fetishes of love
and spread them willy-nilly on the concrete.

# Poem

I believe I am something great.
Otherwise I lost all I gave.
Why should I have complained about love?
Love drove on and realized its own passion.
I hate Ezra Pound.
They all come around me and don't understand—
The leech of the century—love can't
prosecute the BIG TEACHER? HE is
probably the original sin personified (hatred of the self
in the form of mother love). Howard, Howard, why
did you do this to me? A city is a factory. A bridge
removes the obstacle to love, a lone soul is a tunnel, I
asked my mother for a prayer-book—she is made of goodbyes,
I had a father that died of God's wish—
I have a mother that lingers through my soul.

# The Long Leaping Rabbit

Eyes into focus smiling eyes
Rear end of a jackass
The short end of a long leaping rabbit
It's all the same
No matter whose metaphor
I always call a whore a whore
Sherry eyes blotching the bible

Paste or plastic
Painted by Hindemith
Common or drastic
It's all the same
No matter whose rhetoric

Eyes that outlive the body transgress the brain
How long do they live?
Long as the battery?
Long as the short end of the long leaping rabbit
It's all the same
No matter whose eyes
Gaze at booze may rise like
Thighs like the short end of the long leaping rabbit

## watching mother

little by little
she breathes
        less and less
    after a while
she stops
        gets up
                whews!
and breathes again

walks her bending shoulders
to the window
            and lets some air in

seeing her there
            beaten by time
in her Indian silence
            with her Negro dowry
drawing pictures on the window pane
with the ball of her first index finger . . .

## Poem

I sucked her out of a hole in an orange
She had seeds sticking to her very wet body
When I spit her out she fell with a tiny ping down
On a sedentary cloud.
With her lips flapping open and shut
She requested me to lift her up
And slipshod I scooted slumplike to see her close
Exuding damp sprays of sun-dipped gold
The cloud was raising its misty greyness and she was crying
So I lifted her up with her gold splashing and painting me
As the cloud rose high, high, then precipitated down
In tiny raindrops washing us clean, melting a hole
For us to stand, waist deep in water to watch the sun leave

# Model at Her Mirror

A jaded jar,
filled with burning sun,
leans forward,
pouring into a cool smooth blue lake
Princess Orange, sitting on her orange blossom throne,
smiles on herself in the water.

Burning red hair falls into the sun,
crackling, then flows around her face,
when she lifts it leaning back upon her throne.

Her blushing eyes are kissed by eels
as she leans forward pouring, pouring
orange powder into the water
as freckles cleaving her face
drift through a sad solitary cloud
which now splatters laughing, laughing
as pearls trill her fingers
sprinkling the red panorama of her mouth.

Shall we show her an orange blossom
and say it splashes out its pollen into the sun
like her face erupts the molten red veins of her soul
as it dangles in the silvery glasslight water?

Her hair burns red and falls into the sun,
crackling, then falls around her face,
when she lifts it leaning back upon her throne.

## To Love, Quietly: a Novelette

To love softly, with a feather spring, in the walk, in the way you speak, as I will talk to you on this day of sundry sunshine and effervescing clouds, this melancholic afternoon, near the end of spring, cuckolding summer slipping hither from yon promonotorious mountain.

To softly say those things that thunderously bellow in the heart. Quietly sitting beneath some definite thing as a tree laying its leaves along the warm air of a pastoral afternoon protects with shade the tender thinking you have to do, you must have to do.

To move quietly, on the meadow grass, where the tender ends of tree branches have nearly touched, when the powerful oceanic winds of the sky have bent their strong arms, hither thither, and whipped at their barely moving trunks standing strongly wavering in their innermost parts, moving ever so softly, in strength, whispering from bellowing tender thoughts, which I turn to simple words of love I give to you.

Of the tree moving in its own stillness, we build grandeur. Of this instant memory, quiet longing, dying sadness moving heavily on sturdy legs over this pastoral birthing, we build love. Love and grandeur! Of mobile frustration and home-grown long-groomed gloom and utter nonchalance, we fashion a man, drenched in sunshine, to his brown bones. Of this brown man, drenched in sunshine, reaching for this brown girl, wrapped in afternoon's tenderly embarrassed foliage we fashion love.

## Poem

Forget her
I have longed to roam the sun
I would forage her heart only
She would be lost
The sky would descend
I could never forget her
I would have a beggar heart
I would steal my own longing
I would swallow the sun.

Remember her
I don't believe she really cared
I will give her my heart to see if it is really so
She fumbles the ball
She stands on a tower proclaiming
God knows what
God knows what she proclaims
I lost my heart
I turned to pass the ball to her
She turned to blend her belonging
She bent to smell the salt sea air
When the earth belched up from its unlearned abyss.

# Poem

Seems silly to quibble with silver and dream of flowing waters.

Come as drenching rain through the aftermath of the divided spirit.

Cling to me when the train stops to turn on all its faucets.

The screaming wheels of the locomotive dwindle to a stop and sigh.

Not the breath of an angel or a saint but that of a quiet night.

We shall stick a pin in the universe and no one shall squeeze it into a ball.

Don't you know I loved you since I first saw you struggling to build your fire darling.

Let us go in to sleep and dream in the dark saliva of God.

Fought gained lost the trial and loved lost and won the deal and died.

Please . . . please consider the dream and laugh at the fallen buzzard.

We have been taken by the bite of the transient Mephistopheles.

And cling to the sides of the passages that lead down to hell.

Clutch cling I bang and yell and the devils ring the bells

Wells of loneliness fill with the torn flesh of human cells

We slide through slime as rich and red and orange as our souls wonderfully.

Cuddle up to me darling let's sit by the fire and make jokes.

Let's laugh at the twinkling eyes of night and pretend we are just as happy about it as they are.

Sit with me and let the firelight that we make trample on the feet of winter.

Let the bosses sing us an old song before we trip them on the rose bush.
We got lost from each other on the first day and have not really found the way yet.
Give us an idea of where it is and we will ask for it politely.
If she ever sees where I am now she will give up in despair.
We are sitting on opposite sides of the world and it is turning in the gloaming.
While the sky is turning too detached and independently various in its moods.

## Tree Love

When it was not it was, and now that it is
It is not the murmur from the sky that I
Hear in the purpose of my blood. Red blood
Floating in a chasm in the air, singing
The song of cannot ever achieve a successful stopping
And brag about it. A tree meets me in my doorway.
It is a sap tree of the Orient. I hug it; kiss it; fondle
Its leaves in my hands,—talk to it. It can never be:
One forming one's own destiny. I see tiny vines growing
Out to me. I dance with my tree in the moonlight.

## Who I am

Kunzite
kissing bug
loud night
my kit of mornings safely tucked away
dolphin of my heart
. . . swim
kissing bug
O my martingales of laughter
. . . find me
here where I hide laughing even at you
ugly mind
dome of Santa Maria della Salute, Venice
things swell like this eternal doomsday
. . . delighting me
you have an idea who I am now, do you not
kissing bug
loud night
my day's dolphin drifting thru the west

## dolphin is tradition

when one swims out of breath
and looms a patch of floating leaves
one turns on the last energy to overcome
the swirling float of castoff eyes of nonchalance.

when one grabs at floating leaves
and gloom returns with the sinking palms
hiding places of mirth turn with their wet daggers
and rip our lungs to shreds.

dolphin is tradition, like love, and wild wishing!

## Poem

butterflies
suspend her
in air
and off she is flown
to never never land
        my stomach
turned inside out
is in what you may call rapture

you see I fancy poetry

yes, she is a rapture
—ultra real
only saw her once
        when she looked
      now she looks
    looks like migrating birds
           gone away
          gone far away
        gone to never never land
             ultra real land

yes she is a rapture
is what you may call a rapture

## Poem

Life is like a ritzy tower when all the people have gone home
Down in the basement the worms nibble at the steel girders
Tears attend the crumbs left and give them back gleefully
Our room has all the draperies drawn and the bed is made up
When you left ahead of me I stood in the open doorway and watched you disappear
Cold winter when the ritzy tower is emptied of all your flesh
I can't feel the cold but can see the trees glassed in frost
The fish are frozen in the lake and the squirrels hang dead by their tails
The air blends its cold waters with the cold gold sunshine

We're frozen in this large crystal ball universe
When one huge blow of the sledge hammer swings and we crack
Murmurs rise from the slosh and breathing prayers rise
An egg-beater is inserted and we are broken and stirred
And when we are even and fluffy and quiet a gavel sounds
"Hear ye! Hear ye! Who has not desired to fornicate?"
No sound from the whipped cream . . . no sound!

## Poem

Nautical fortune balanced word on word
Find diamonds hiding centers and roofs of love.
Tell them forevers grow and blend blooming blisters and
Repetitious forget-me-nots.

Night noise to morning glories
Awaken the will-of-the-wisp, his night
Is never ending toil, a multiple-tongued liar
Doomed to gather the ashes of the burning sky,
Both day and night, fortunes aftermaths
Beginning.

Darkness of light lay dull liars in gullies where angel tears stream,
Reawaken your blending, build your rebirth, grow and gather
Little things like far-away stars into your bursting heart
Of light grinning through bursting balloons and popping souls
Beginning glory.

Tented light open your flaps and let out your song
Thelonious Monk
Disdains noxema.

TOM POSTELL

## Of Bettie

Can we know when to see and when not to see
Can we know when to tell the world to stop
Yes we know when to rise and when to fall
Yes we know when to sit and warble bird songs

I went to the sea to ask God what to do
And he told me to stand in the middle of the deepest part
To stand in the drain when her tears would try to escape
To gather them like pollen and take it back to the flower they came from

I told God to go to hell and try that on the devil
And he listened and ran back a little and ran back to me and stood there
I told God that I would not gather her tears like they were pollen
For they were and are the juice from her eyes which now are sad

I love her like the sun loves the flowers and the sea and all of us
I told God all this and he listened with his ear to the ground for Satan
Was on his way to claim his brother and his brother was waiting in vain
For the sea and the sun to cull the sap from our souls and preach it green

I love her like the sea and the flowers and the wind kissing the flowers
I love her like cars love roads and the roads love the land and the sky
I love her like the North Pole loves the South Pole
And she loves me drastically as zero

## Poem

let us unwind the alarm before morning peeps over
                                        yesterday's dipsydoodles
let us wring the chicken's neck sadly
                                unreverberating

—it's so unorthodox
martian small pox
yesterday the iceman came
(with a load of forget-me-nots)
egrets of loneliness flew through
                                her deepest regrets
telegrams from LeRoi Jones to the judge made my right hand it
the bitch, the bitchfull, undone baloney, long pauses
                        and thirty-five minutes a line of brains
and why in the name of reason did we prop up our tent

it's orthodox and reverberating
television free on board your land-locked canoe
and the terrible story to tell today hides in growing tree limbs
I don't take any credit for my clean laundry
any laundryman would have done it
my mother doesn't give a damn either
she and I planned the whole thing
the theater manager did it for charity
my father died to mold our glory
Uncle Sam bought long and sold short
and the rest of us stood up and coughed

We all have a cold
Let us retire and tend to it

## Poem

Yon dog: are you god?
Well then stand on your nose;
Stand on your curly tail.
You are John Keats past twenty-five years of age
Passing on your way to Troy:
Mangy cur, spots of shiny blue
You are the hump in the tree.
Here comes the law from a bush
With a tall oak stick for me.
Like a rolled up rejection slip.
But, mangy cur, did you run?
No wonder—cops everywhere,
Even in the axle of the leaf.
Yon dog turned tail: are you god?

## Poem

Midst mornings of arrivals our love grew.
Now in night's black block of ice that love dies.
Reality is my heart.

I chained my words and hid them in my soul,—
my eyes their only windows.
You saw and sorted out our moments from the unhappy throng
and we went where the wind blows.

Our looks were streets upon which our love drove.
To touch was as jolting to our hearts as automobiles colliding.
Sadness was our start and now our own dead end.
And between the poles our lips met in resurrection.

It was nearly morning.
I bought a rose and ate it.
I climbed upon a roof and waited.
You came then left without a warning
Our souls were never sated.

Sirens of my sighs from the abyss.
At last memory is my chosen friend.

## Poem

boy
you thought you were white
something we never dreamed of
now you say you are whole
now you realize you are black
—black maybe
you are telling white people
now you have seen the light
still waiting for them to pat your back
pat your back . . . humh
now they will have to deal with you on your own terms
now that you speak for a nation
and not yourself
boy
look into your heart
now you have done it
they patted your back once
for all it was worth
you with your knife
stuck into my back
all the more pain
yew kin fergit it
though
they are just what you say they are
and there must be war
and you are just what your are
Gunga Din
telling them which way we are coming
now we will have to come by way of the river
dragging our hooks in the water

## Love Boat

If there are such things as love
Lift them from my gloom and let them glow
If there are no such things
Touch me and hear my song

Doooh, here we go, and Tina
Lifting star bulbs from my brain
Faaah, thou Tina, lovely Tina
So, my, me, so my O my tinatinatina

In truth we go
To it to whoooo
Slowly
Row our boat dohdoh

Doooh, here we go, and Tina
Sprinkling star dust on love's terrain
Faaah, thou Tina, lovely Tina
So, my, me, so my O my tinatinatina

This star heart ticks love
For you

In truth we go
To whit to whoo whoo
Slowly row our boat
Great witch of love
Doh re mi fa so

Throw me back
Or don't rock the boat

Tina, out of this take me
Row, row our boat
Gently through the currents
Gently
Listen to me
We cannot stop

Things you recognize, take,
Others, accept for awhile,
Listen for things that bind us together,
Offer, as emblem to my symbols,
Your audio and visio beauties, watch and listen
Like you offered your body
That I took with such fervor
With the tenderness of Jesus arms and legs
Until such fervor bubbled from below
Into your softly very being, your warmth-
My arms and legs roamed all your soft valleys
While my fervor bubbled and burst

Throw me back
Or quit rocking the boat

Sit down and
And listen to me
We cannot stop

Things you recognize, take,
Those you don't, offer
To my fervor
I lay among your soft valleys
If there are such things as love

Lift them from my gloom and let them glow
If there are no such things
Touch me and hear my song

Night drifts widely from my gloom
Fills my room
A lone star glows
That's Tina, That's Tina

Tina tiptoes thru my room
Searches for the leisure of my gloom
Flip flop it's unsidedown
See it flounder
Wrap its wings around my gloom
Then words come bellowing about my room
"Fumbler. Full blown balloon head.
"Raise your head. Look up there.
"She's just standing there, up there
"Leaning down.
"Watch out!
"She will kiss you."

Don't kiss me now
But hear my song

If there are such things as love
Lift them from my gloom and let them glow
If there are no such things
Touch me and hear my song
Morning starlight Tina
Evening starlight Tina
Limelight
Dancelight
Sweet Georgia Brown
That's Tina, That's Tina
Two say Tini
And those I love too

That's our business who they are
They're she they're me
We're they they're we
Honeycomb
—they're her sweetness

Things you recognize, take,
Others, accept,
Listen for things that bind us together
Offer as emblem
The body
I took with such fervor,
Your tender flesh I took
Your tender sighs I took
The boat knocks against the shore
And slips again to drifts that
Swiftly join the currents moving
Backwards though they swell forward
With the welter of my love spreading
Foamly, so lovely Tina

She said to filter out her truths
And I did to pamper her
Long before she asked
Replaced them with my lies
And buried all that stuff
Hugged her to my breast
Emptied the stream and filled it with my thought
Placed pillow forward in the boat
Folded the sky and laid down my head
With Tina's

God damned us
· And set us adrift
And here we go
Aglow

# Sandra

Past lives' loads gather growling while wily were-wolves chew us
In the evening of a picnic stroll, when Satan turns out all the fires.
The night that loves us so much tears out our hearts while we sleep. Cool
Moon . . . moon. You see only the outline of the turning dead queen of joy.
Black sky of unblemished sin, pure, all black bone round the big eye shut us up
Sandra, tears wander from wild eyes, and curse the old twisted trunks of age . . .
Turning green world, rollicking in grief, round aspirin of love, dangerous discovery,
Breaking beginning of blame, cement of our own town cornerstone, blooming evening wallflower . . .
—don't let us gather only to drink—let's wallow in the wind,
Let's blend into the afternoon, let's lay in the sun's arms happily dreaming,
Let's turn over and sigh.
Oh love    mother of bloom    drinker that sits at the well    oh love
Sandra, Sandra, debts are never paid. Hides only gather at conventions of bus stops,
Nights without ever opening to ever-lighting-blasting stars twirling into hearts,
Drone, consume the floating wild heart, cast for the beginning again, all hail!

## Poem

blue, has-been moons cry-blasting barrels of wings,
she came and sat near the cold clear well;
light blue, the sky turned over and buzzards dropped down.
Bright glass eyes watched as we sat, honeydew
sadness laughed, people peeped into our clear window.
gray building as heavy as a wood roof of love,
the trained morning of our song-heaven enshrouded,
cumbersome as love arms we climbed each other
into a loft of hair, sparrows sat, butterflies hesitated.
she knew before I told her, numbers of eternity
one breath of the winds, sing-song love, fire.

## The Laments of a Poor Poet

I sit around all day thinking of love
A piece of gold dangling by a silken cord
While the water runs over Niagara Falls
And the lovers kiss in the misty sprays
My mother sits hungry in the other room
Head between her knees, hair uncombed
The old poets are off somewhere eating sides of beef
Having won their award
There is an old bottle of wine in the cupboard
My love is off holding thighs
If I work, I am too tired to write
If I write, I starve, I'll stand beneath the sky
And curse God

# Dancing on Stone

Eating cantaloupe
On the curbstone
Laughing and chewing
What an American grin
Chews cantaloupe
On the rusted concrete curbstone
He doesn't care about the rags
This child too young
To have been to a prom
He only looks about himself grinning
Swallowing the juicy taste of cantaloupe
He is not black or white or green
But child: the unsuspecting race
Richer than Rich
Appreciating cantaloupe
Found in a garbage can
Taking the strange extra sweetness
Of rotting fruit
Into his tiny mouth
Gurgly laughing
Dancing his feet on stone

## Even if

These Bardic Days churning light upon the loam,
trundel the sky. So we lie immersed in foam,
drumming sadness into rocks, and crying lakes. And after
noon air lifts robins, lifts their wings away up there.
No. No. Don't form dark clouds in my sky this day.
Nor this night when sleek lanes lead to the moon's lambent glades.
Where drunken Gods whittle seriousness into willows falling to their knees,
their trembling knees that rock the mud and foam
until daylight shakes with laughter laughing and then wanes when
love parks among these shadows seducing white lightning . . .
This vague blues floats over a bridge with sorrowful foundations.
Our knees are trembling holding up the vibrating mountain
while angels dance through these dreams whispering love words
among the crumbling sands trickling through the hands of the meadow clocks.
People lead sheep horses cows, and robins lift lofty things and songs and poets,
and indifference opens filling stations so my dark love can drive these pick-up
trucks of words worn dumb for Christ. O lackadaisicallity vibrating
pedantically over the settlement of these dreams descend

dumbly to her token heart and stagger through that gloom dying
like the doubt buried in the plans God made for the unworthy.
When it was the time of awakening these words bobbed from her heart to my heart
spawning jack-o-lanterns springing from high places telling dirty jokes and
poking fun at the whole project like sound is harmony and meaning is
woe-begotten and darkness is God turned inside-out for sorrow and sin.
When I told them to lay down the runway they all yelled for popcorn
and I went to the outdoor john laughing to beat the band and it was
Alexander's Ragtime Band and the crowd cheered when we landed singing
The Star Spangled Banner. O O O O O they will never dig
the grave of a real American even if they try their dirty work on Sunday.

# The Green Rose

Plan on ashtrays with silver linings
if you have half a heart.
With the moon turning behind your back
don't forget to sing.
The heart of a hobo burns
for fever of children's endless Abaddon.
Years turn cartwheels with Christmas trees and fireflies
flapping on the brain.
Sad light approaches illuminating gray clouds
and the mutilated human terrain.
Terrestrial sorrow and organic disaster
deflate this ignominy of universe.
We win prizes for running around the rainbow
faster than its colors diffuse.
With your willow-while come
within the smoke of my whisper and kneel down.
Shoot dice like rabbits chase the core of most private thoug
O halo mine!
Pulsating halo twist around Saint Peter's
cathedral tower at moon-high midnight then
burn sun day burn sun O burn sun daylight
O bright daylight of the Roman Candle.

## Poem

Ta dum ta dum
to you a hum
one run and one walk
stalk

Ta dum ta dum
bun bun

Who shoo who shoo
one boo boo
owl
wipe it

Psycho
ta dum ta dum

without a song . . .
. . .

Who shoo
boo boo
biddledebum
psycho

shoo it
to it
boo it
wipe it

three guesses

referee
free these
hang those
suppose the wind shifted
. . . who knows
suffer
druther
bell and tell
shit
its own name

Ta dum ta dum

# Gertrude Stein Rides the Torn Down El

*—to New York City*

Then colors rose through the leaves in light
      surprise.
The last peacock poised and sighed on the leaves
      and rose.
Wonderful day careens while blighted riffraff
      children skate and
Laughingly dig the hole for the mid-western
      bonfire.
Wrap honey in velvet air and hide it in October's
      searching breath.
The bonfire dwindles as the circus leaves and
      the animals roar.
It's only in the sun that madness splatters into
      joy . . .
Cover down the moon for the night before you
      lift the skirts of a cloud.
Love knocks on the inside of my skull and kicks
      in my stomach.
A doe licks the gum from a tree and runs into
      the woods.
She lets me govern her gaze when the parade
      blares its colors.
Gertrude Stein is long dead but under cover rides
      the torn down El.

## Glass Balls Roll off a Dome in the Sky onto the White Marble Dance Pavilion

*—with the left eye on the bomb*
*and the right one on my girl*

I have known for some time the heaven
where race horses are losing themselves.
The finishing post from the rail would lean in wonder
if it could tell time.
Turning on all the faucets in the automat
I floated through the revolving doors reposed.
When the wind sneaks under morning's cover
and settles on your books don't laugh.
Wonderful leaves chasing a horde of jellybeans
clutching her last five cents.
Jazz blues moves like electricity
gifting bodies with grandiose histrionics.
I can't help it if they caught her that morning
and melted her into a puddle of love.
Mapping morning hating morning our love
O I don't care about our love until
Glass balls roll off a dome in the sky
onto the white marble dance pavilion.

# Once upon a Time I Was a Sober Fox . . . . .

Once I was sober
as a fox in a refrigerator
three weeks and twice as anti-social
when I thought how I was deluded and decided
to rebel.  Unable to move, I sat still watching
violence open the door to get a soda-pop or some
ham and eggs. After the door closed and clicked dutifully, in the
dark, I ran my fingers through my hair.

Once I played and danced in green
fields among colored flowers and trees
that looked at God all day. Then over
rolling hills swung the yellow sun and burst into
thunder of heaven and came yelping devils, and I ran,
thinking it a game I might somehow win.

Once upon a time they caught me,
sank their teeth into my flesh, like
thorns turning upon the rose. I run my fingers
through my hair.  In the dark. When will they
decide to eat me? I am living beyond my death!

Once I carried two daggers in my
hands! I carried two daggers to slash
the intestines of the night! The daggers
turned into bottles of pale dry sherry, and I
drink!

The sherry pours down my throat and I
jump and turn cartwheels in the dark, like tumbleweed when the moon
   is down.

# WXYZ

anything for a poem
cut wrists
all things lay down before the poem
o lord your head is blowing up
chop chop green tree for a poem chop chop
myself child I love so very much drop dead
for a poem I will stand on my own two feet for awhile
for a poem I will give up black white but not green women
i'll lay my head in green bower swilling it very good
but not virtue i'll not give up this virtue you can plainly see
o bald feet trespassing footfalls of lollipopian shakespeares roam
doom is dumb and to be too soon is sorrow and too too is splash splash
sooooooooooooooooooogreeeeeegooooooorrrrrrrrrrie slops slops
the world is not a beat beat but a bang bang and a blown-up balloon
a strung green words and lanterns along love's grove and moved over time
a stood up and dewigged grew a beard for tomorrow shall be sad
b lives among green trees with a broken heart
b will not sing again will not greet spring again or build fire again, either
b is full of shit as a christmas turkey
c is happy and swims in a silver puddle of water
c is a harpy with golden wings
the rest is defghijklmnopqrstuv and you can sell it on the open market

Uncollected Poems
(1950–1980)

*In addition to what Rose Bianchi and the Editors consider to be his singular finalized manuscript* The Tomb, *Postell left a number of undated drafts (some of which exist in duplicate as retyped by Bianchi on a word processor) as well as a typescript for a longer, generative process-work titled* Seasons. *In that typescript, Postell declares "I have written only one book of poems, it was called* The Tomb"; Seasons, *by Tom's own sarcastic estimate, "would take five years to polish." Bianchi's conversations with Postell testify to the context of its genesis.*

Seasons *contains 132 consecutive "opuses" dated from Spring 1975 to Winter of 1976, Postell's best intention being to write a poem every day. Loose drafts of undated poems were discovered by Bianchi in a small cardboard box after Postell's death in 1980. A "typo-pathology" is challenging, though we can note Postell's usage of two to three different typewriters (one quite early, one middle-period machine closely matching that used to compose* Tomb, *and one later machine co-owned by Postell and Bianchi). Nevertheless, aside from the opuses of* Seasons, *we cannot ascribe dates to these poems with any certainty.*

*The Editors have taken few liberties with the transcriptions of these poems—works which present themselves as either finished or as ready-for-final-typing. Only obvious cases of misspelling and typographical error were corrected, with berth given to Postell's often idiosyncratic formatting, dialect, and concrete "play." In all cases they appear just as Tom left them. —Eds.*

## Harmony

We who stung stone know how our toil bathed us in ash, while lilies of the land covered their heads and shuttered. We had grass blades for legs and tree limbs for arms and our mouths were big black clouds, which at times would burst warnings to civilizations.

We remember the times we were nearly human, and almost understood the caresses of fried fish laced around our groins by ambassador girl diplomats from the sorry state of God.

You and I were the wine glass tasting the wine but swallowing none. Sitting on the forgotten table of love. We looked in our own eyes and blinked stars the moons were jealous of.

I loved you under the crushing sledge of wrath, of morning's pressure on the heat of evening. Moons and secrets.

# ˈideo

hite people taking baths
sing ivory soap cause it so pure
osing on video picture tubes for union scales
ater dripping from their hairy white skin
r the stockholders the presidents and the man on the street
hite people chewing gum and brushing their teeth
eaning the germs in public and tossing them into the drains
ey the germs swim play and return to their white masters again
ctra! extra! read all about how clean white people are
eautiful white girls combing their hair in public
r table stakes the video lets you play and it's ten to one
e white man with two dabs in his hair will get the silver girl
d if nothing else works then change your deodorant
e shaves with the latest roller blades or uses cream
's dashing and debonair she's the lily of the valley
ne it in better see how they glow they are the kind of people likes people
ru the video they come so sweet so smooth so lovely
tween the gunfighters and the doctors and the private eyes
ing turned off being turned on by the flick of my fingers
who am nothing and have no power at all
who use the same two-ply facial tissue

## A Fecundation

Kissing

    her                                        sun

   was          ..                          calm

     like                      a

       sticking       into

          my tongue

For I        her passion    a thoroughbred

   controlled          like           horseman

          black night

      filthy

     her into     comet               inside her

   I rode       a            rumbling

And          like      thundering

    whinning     me

Her

         and                entertwined

    lightning     a       tail         and

And            comet's              made fireflies

## Poem

Heckling speckling past, O joyous
Prancing lips, O ranting time

Nice glowing eyes, O smiling tirade
Of teeth, O whispering cheeks of bronze

Speaking tongues, O vocal golden cords
Sing loud, O chant my beaconing, O
Chant my beaconing

# Poem

Roy Baby
listen to me
remember when I told you about the bastards
remember how much I drank
did we both know about ambivalence
I did and you do now I'll lay it on them
one told me it was just a game
stole our pot of gold and spit in my face
and you were quiet for awhile but baby you're not quiet now
come to think of it though you told in the beginning what you would do
Roy dad when they took it with their money and papermill I felt like Cane
I would have liked to be polite about it but that would have been hammy
shit the bastards have not stolen anything at all
now let them go to jail for something they didn't do
like the poor wino on the street they lock up while the big thieves go free
are respected members of the community and even get to be president
one major criminal here said my poems were not original
I have imitated the beatniks you know the poems I had when you told me about

what I should read because I had not read that fellow and I should do it

Man we told each other things and neither of us listened

to whit to who tho he too doo doo and let them woo woo their whammy mammy

their druthers stunk and academic bric-a-brac tied their tongues together

remember when I hugged you in Washington Park and told you I loved you

it would have been more polite to say I understood and shake your hand

if the beautiful ones put each other down I'll put you down, didn't you know

I am a conformist

remember when you would throw me out of the window

you could have too

what are poets made of

sugar and spice but superman could not have thrown me out of that window

what are poets made of is what I told you in Washington Park

I hope I don't run out of paper before I finish

to us to them these things have different meanings and glad tidings laugh

let me except Lila and Henue and you can gather and love as many French people

as I do and you can't get all of them into a bag that human hands made

let them drop and burst like the love our country demanded us to give

and withdraw to the place where decision turns the mind to stone.

## Opus 12

They're dying left and right. Or else the young are still-born.
Only the black poets are living, having things to say.
The awful stench of corpses stifle the daylight hours.
Only at night when we are all sleeping, in the kitchen of my desir
Can I cook rose leaves, smell their soft fragrance, and return
To eat the raw ones, hoping the sap will flow thru my veins.

I grip my pen in my black hand searching for clear images
That throb with life. None come and I must humble myself
To read Don L. or Ameer and wallow in their lifeblood.

There is a literary revolt loose on the sands of America—
Black brothers with pen or quill giving it to the white man.
Wild ecstatic voices, and the sisters too are singing. Sonia
And Stephany and so many black brothers and sisters singing
In places we don't know of. What we see is only the tip of the iceb

What the white man sees is his ship going down—
With many good souls aboard. It's tragic everytime
The wind shifts and new voices are heard—first the
Destructive diatribe and then a sweet new voice like Stephany's
Or a sweet old voice like Mason Jordan Mason.

O all the voices are sweet and music to my ears.
The white man howling as his ship goes down
The black man coming out of earth like a rose
To kiss the sun O the new day has come
The world is
drip-
ping

with
new
life

O Ethiopia O Egypt O long standing Orient
The seeds are harvesting all over
The moon pulls forth sap that in sunlight blooms
A new day wakens all my brothers, white and black
To the timely fact that it is the black man's day
The ribbon is broken, let the ship slide down its way.

# I Make a Pact with You LeRoi Jones
# I Have Ignored You Long Enough

without effort
the songs have gone
filled with outwitted deformities of social disgrace
gone to use burned in fires of rejection slips
not quite the equal of humanity of a computer machine
—bah! and fi; or is it fe, fi, fo, fum, but anyway, bah! bah! baby . . .
gone to the most inner circle of hell, without favor outside it,
therefore garbage cans ignored them gutter winds shoved them

       along without effort the songs have gone
chilled into facelessness of statues windsanded a thousand years
into illness no doctor dare dig into with a sniff or a laugh
—this life
terror has dwindled, only pain and boredom tear away the skin
of what was love.

This poem was blended in Scotland and bottled in Cincinnati.
But you can open it where you please, and you can go to hell too.

Without a notch the gun falls back into place.
Open your ears and close your heart
for tomorrow is a cloud of heartburn and lies
doctors in dirty dungarees digging tanks for liquid cornerstones.
       Silly pink spots withering on the wall, sound gathering itsel
And gathered non-love relaxes on the terrace of beloving,
—mean measures, rhythms catch and hold, gathered days gather
gone lines and laughter, children pick sitting birds, neon
non-love, relax on the terrace of beloving, words unstring me!
And who cares about spring relaxes thru the winter in scotch
scotch-tape this and send it to your grand-daddy.

## Poem

To be dead is to live because you must live to die.
When you are no longer dead then you have never lived.
When you have never lived then you can have faith in God.
When you have faith in God then he will make you an ant.
When you are an ant you can preach.
Because then you know, —Ho! Preach me a sermon.
Ant! Tell me how happy you are there carrying that crumb.
It is not enough for me to eat so don't offer me any.
Just tell me of your passions, your views on Freud.
Ant eat
ter coming over the hill—, run preacher, run.
Here the anteater is the wind by the windmill.
It is cer
tain that peace
is not death.

Since like death carrying this further would be un-
comfortable I will end it knowing there is more to do.

## Poem

LIGHT!

catching the bulbs

of insatiable steam

YES!

Have seen him in smoky rooms

With the lit red lights of his eyes

Caught on parakeets' wings

Piercing the velvet hide of night

Out where the moon

pours lemonade

on our black souls

as we turn with

Parker's eyes

looking aslant at

maybe a rose

or a cop in the doorway

ANNOUNCING GOD

## Two Minus One

The day of darkness
Ridden lightbulb dinosaurs
Martian phantasmogoria

Black on black or bric-a-brac
Stack on stack or was is was is
He denounces the painter
He announces (the painter)
Antecedent invisibilities

Black on black or bric-a-brac
Antecedent invisibilities

He'll never know
Sunken eyes of his drunken sot
Never know the looks her lover got
Never know
The day of darkness

## Poem

What is it I hear?
Where do I go? The birds
fall over in sorcery,
over the fall silvery dropping,
as the bells in the high steeple on the hill
clang up in the clouds,
as sand in wine
explodes in the angel's eyes.
Yes! We cry in the glades of eyelash
blurring the vision in the fish pond
of diamond fish at midnoon,
poured on this sad metropolis
which is a city in the deep sea,
which is a drop of ink in the balls of Christ
as he pounces on the pile of barbed wire
and fires his gun.

# Typescripts
## (1950–1980)

*Typescripts here are presented as scans of Postell's extant manuscripts as kept by Rose Bianchi and archived in the Elliston Poetry Collection at the University of Cincinnati. They are drawn primarily from Postell's uncollected drafts and the opuses of* Seasons, *and as such comprise writing between approximately 1950 and 1980. They have been chosen to provide readers a.) some vantage of Postell's work habits on the page, and b.) a sense of material left by Postell in varying states of incompletion or draft. Though this is a visual retrospect, we hope the inclusions also give readers a sense of Postell's evolving subject matter and attitude. —Eds.*

# THE RIVERBOAT GAMBLER

I chopped moon rocks, with

the blunt edge on old ink-pens, I found

discarded by golf greats on old green country clubs, they built

on the flaoting islands they tried to dam the river with, oh

I dug a hole to threw the rocks down into, and posed, rocks in hands,
        dropping them,
one by one, like I learned from French poetry, giving them their heaving
        freedom, divorcing them, as they plummetted
through swollen threats, splashing, of birds flying up from hell, I told

the hole was too much like a pussy, the rocks too existing, flailing lik
        shadow of Christ, on our loved ones, I
wound the springs of the clock so tight they can never move again, I rub
        my shoulders and buttocks against the clock works, she
told me Paris was love and New york was money, I trailed her with a weep
        willow swishing like a tail, I
ruined legions of port wine, cast their frames to the garbage cans, ripp
        out seams that bound my soul, I
dialed long distance operators all over the world and told them I am a
        Negro, I
aung up before they could answer, except for Copenhagen, Copenhagen, I
        heard no sound from Copenhagen, they said Kierkegaard was dead now
not want to hear the world comment on me, even Copenhagen, even Martiniqu
        while Cesaire spins his black top in Paris, without me, I
watched television with tongue in cheek, listening to the fools laugh
        climbing from the hole in the ground, I
dropped rocks one by one, they fell with disdain

and struck bland brains that sang, the mad

woman I met burning old gossip columns buttoned my shirt, I

told her that the sea was to ~~blame.~~ blame.

And she believed me.

# CANTOSANITY

Yet say this to Jack Kerouac

cats are only drooping they don't sleep

ever try one out daddy-yo

lets you and I go

down to Baltimo

where your daddy

and your mammy

don't know how to say

dis and dat and dese and does


one night to go

where the river flows

perfect meditation

black and full of trash

like my gaze and yours

sunsets and dooryards

gates and sleepy lagoons

bafoons and bards

let us not speak of saddness

-it speaks too much of itself a lone

let us throw the dogaa bone

and blow up a baloon

and bloom inmeditation

a condone full of the void

and float far over horizons

of fear

and sing and also bring

back the words they threw away

when they married the bankers

and locked up our hearts

and sold the securities for the accessories

and said that is all they need


O kill me dead

in quotes

in neon lights

headlines

or just tell my mother the truth

I have waited a long time for this

it is mean of me to say it

but is it so

down in Baltimo

that the fish just skip it

and the sea horse does not give a dam

I don't believe it though

even of Baltimo

and poor old John Kasper

blind, blind as a bat

can you imagine Allen @insburg fat


I have a lot of things I am going to say

before I move on to greener pastures

you can eat my haylofts behind me

earchy of heaven, silver  leaves of her mirror, dream wings of birds, dreams, dreams-
ng as a road and beginning as love, silver leaves grow wings in the catching air.

ooms of fingers wander in my hair; feather flung ideas cling and clutch; her hippodrome of
                                                              floating
arlet hair. The west wind turns to her for a kiss, gliding feathers of my breath, can I be
                                                              it?
r blends into her shoulders, eyes come out of black and white light, water running over
                                        gold skin is her afternoon.
ack light of dreams, lofty winging minds,love trudging its way through the sky, bars jaili
                                                    romance,

ads dethroned, deep sea shadows, oh girl, oh girl, romance, armed with moths I standing
                                    scream and stand up, upward.
ky filling with balloons cries as a formation of angels descend smilling, crying teardrop
                                    of pearls. Singing.


lous of the sea, land turns to the mountains and becons the rivers.
I slip between the foilage of my love's eyes and go to sleep.

I hear voices inside me making inaudible pleas which I think are for freedom
mingling with the pulsing blood and flooding organs they know how unsplitable
                                                    the skin is as I do
The disorder inside me increases with fatigue and the tissues weaken
Perhaps the little men inside my rotting carcus think that fatigue is a good
                                                    time for them to escape
It doesn't worry me I lay down and sleep
Oh what hell I dream when the disorders of the day focus moving pictures on
                                                    black screen

Closing doors turn into a roaring flood
Stop and go signs rip the fleash from my skin
Iron bars deluge the the raw bones and loose organs from the skin
Beautiful women in sail boats skiff through me and dissipear over the
                        horizon laughing laughter dying like a bird climbing
                        up into the sky to swoop down in a glide and the laugh
                        and the beautiful women and the birds drift away to th
                        horizon again


Freedom! Freedom! let my people go
Go down Moses and set my people free
I am too big and green and wet and rocky and obedient
I want to burst! out loose my straining veins
Ignite the thunderbolts piercing my head
I want to sleep an even smooth as smoke sleep
I want to pull the plug out of my clock and spread out dead
Let these little men scatter to their own planets
Confine them no more to the bowl of my brain

*cool*

# POEM

What is I hear?

Where do I go? The birds

fall over in sorcery,

over the fall silvery dropping,

as the bells in the high steeple on the hill

clang up in the clouds,

as sand in wine

explodes in the angel's eyes.

Yes! We cry in the glades of eyelash

bluring the vision in the fish pond

of diamond fish at midnoon,

poured on this sad metropolis

which is a city in the deep sea,

which is a drop of ink in the balls of Christ

as he pounces on the pile of barbed wire

and fires his gun.

# BLUE IS THE COLOR OF SADDNESS

I cling to her hair
She runs after her thought
I sing about her lovelinass
She never denies her plight
I can glean from her this fight
I own this right


She undertakes to kiss the rose
The sound the petals and the lips make
The odd idea that degenerates into a poem
I flutter in the wind afraid
How strong is her love


Intthe morning we run after rivers
The idea of a tear trudging its way through mountains
is a thing that we want to understand
She looks like a tropical storm
I smell like the sea
She has gone and left me
singing the blues


She was a bitch I guess
I dont own anything any longer
When she left me I was numb with pain
The most painful pain is boredom of love
I lost a great deal
My loud cloud was real

I would do anything to make this poem a succe

~~I would do almost anything to make this poem a success~~

...too long...it's been too long
words without pages, songs without spaces
places without names and dates without regard
to homes without faces

...too long...it's been too long
whole books gone
bangs without gongs, sand thru an
hourglass from Coney Island to Jone's Beach
but so long night

ingale
your songs I've never heard
only seen them
in books
( faded shawls of streetwalking women)
sold crooks crude sticks of dynamite
to burst in your cloth bound pussies

...too long...it's been too long

opus 22

After listening to me three years
The honkie was astounded
When I told him Ameer Baraka was the greatest
The truth is I did'nt know until that instant
that he is
He's alive in his blackness struttin for his folks
like a proud black rooster he's all alone
in his glory
the only tranquilizer he needs is to strike the white
man's skull
the olympic games
have refused rhodesia
for what
it goes on all over the world
a little subtler
but more deadly
at least rhodesia does'nt show you something
then jerk it away
like some white jerk told me
in another way
in some long distant time ago
Here it is white man
grab it if you can
I wont jerk it away
but I'll pull you down
and give you your
crown of thorns
like you did
to jesus

Opus 39

(for Etheridge Knight)

ot nature nor meat shall cross my lips today
or symbolic love undressing to my beat
've heard the true song come out to me from night
strong voice from hell rapt in holy vestments
alling the truth with each turn of a phrase
aking me hate the time I wasted digging in white *bags*
now at every turn black shall be my name
lack shall be my avocation churning light upon my loam
hall be my font from which I'll grow my weed
o get high on the sun and not that reflected moonlight shit
s pure a voice as Rilke but not a little lord fontleroy
voice speaking, not yelling, of things dear to him
ore of dear things than dead things a wellspring of love
ocrates did the best job of defining love a movement to it
d Etheridge is a moving van of true (i cant touch it, it moves)
t ice pervades his lines sticking them together
sen't fool around with too much imagery moonlight stuff
metimes he s just a down to earth Cat chanting plain things
bit of a comic immortalizing Shine
king me remember the times we had with the old men of the family
ey told me to stop drinking wine and drink whiskey and I did
t to get in and get out quick keep it moving before the explosion
w to keep it up todate what is he doing now I don't know
t I wont proclaim him dead just because I don't know
don't know nothing while I know he's doing something
proclaim it I proclaim it he's moving always moving
lling tales to the sun who is the God I worship
o will in turn tell them to me

The black man invented potry a long time ago
on walls they painted to help the dead get into heaven.
Now I'm told that the black man is stuck, he can only
write about blackness; only the black poet does not
hear this, he writes as though there were no white poets.
I'm a black man and I know there are plenty white poets
saying things that need be said, that is there were white
poets, all of them have died, and the extant white poets
are extranious, bubbling in blather, singing the song of
nothing. I like Gary Snyder,but with an Ameer Baraka
splicing words together I dont like Gary Snyder- first
things first, and with that young kid Don Lee shouting
all over the place you can not even hear Ginsberg howling.
The true poet sings. Loud. Or soft. But he sings. There is
no such thing as literature in poetry, it's all song, the
black poet sings. What if he sings about the black man and
woman, he sings, goddamit. And when his song is done, he
sings a new song. He sang on the levee and of cotton, he
will sing for you if you would only listen. He's here to
entertain you, why wont you listen? Billie Holiday sang,
and you killed her with your dope. Buried her with your
alcohol during the same time you killed Lester Young, he
loved her, and he sang with his horn, of his love. Charlie
Parker died before his actual death, fooling around with
Greenwich Village, he forgot his roots, they ripped them
up. I got a lot to get off my chest so ease back in your
easychair. I have no hatred, I'm incapable of it, so listen
a little longer. I may be thru a lot sooner than I thot.
I'm getting sleepy. Why should I try to hip you to something

you wont understand anyway. The white man sings of
the white man and the black man sings of the black
man, and you can judge whose song is real. Don L Lee
sings and Allen Ginsberg sings, but whose song is real?
Ginsberg doesnt love the white man, who does Don Lee love?
Judge the poet by his love. Roi doesnt love either, but
he does a good job telling why he doesnt, so does Ginsberg.
My typewriter tells me things. I love it. It makes me remember
what Dudley Randall has done for the black poet! I'd still
be dumb to what black poets are doing, of Sonia, Stephany
and Etheridge are doing, and many others, he is the single
most important poet of this century, kin to Ezra Pound of
the white poets, in just ten short years he has delivered us
from slavery, woke us up to each other, given us a voice.
I hope he doesnt turn into a Booker T., give us freedom to
love, whatever we will love. I love my wife and she loves
my poems, just doesnt like my talking about her dago mother.
I love her mother too. How can you not love a Jean Paul
Satre? We must widen our scope. My wife saved my life so
I can write these poems, and she understands the deadness
of the white man (she wont admit it, tho), but she loves me,
and that is something new to me. And I was not given a nigger
dick either. Mine is just average. I say it's love. No matter
what material I use, if I do it well, she likes it, and
understands it too. She and her brother have no hang-ups
about race, how can I hate them--I love them. I love all
my black brothers and sisters, wether they can read or
write, or just show a brother the short way home.

Summer 1975 Opus 18

The poems come more slowly now
The heat beats earthward through the humidity
Even the telephone poles are sweating their blood
The sun is the lit tip of a cigarette smoked by God
The puffs of clouds are the smoke He blows
I thought the devil was the keeper of the heat
But I know he is far beneath the ground
You really have to work to get to him
For God though you merely have to lay your body down
Let your pores drink the sunshine and get black
Or go dig your hole and meet with the devil
You will need a strong back to dig to hell
It is there though and hotter than the sunlight
Your skin cooks there you'll boil all the way through
The devil will eat you thats what you want dont you
You've got to be a freak to get to hell
What with Jesus forgiving you all your sins
Puff God and rain on us we're children of the sun
Cool us off before the freeze of night
I'll dig a small hole to get You started to the devil
But if you would put out his fire You'll have to dig the rest
You nailed Jesus to the cross before He could dig
I know You with Your carefree ways
You want no more truck with Satan than I do
Send funnel clouds from your smoke
Your journey ends
When Satan comes
Consuming all your children
Leaving you the king of a charred planet

WE SHALL BOAST ANYWAY:
LIKE LOVE I SAY.
                W.H. AUDEN


Give me a window to see out of
I will write you a poem
Open prarie spaces for my longing
I will understand
Turn me over to the cops
I&ll surrender
O turn me over to the cops
I surrender

Give me an Auden idea
Then I will show you
Pull up my shade so I can see
I wont bitch
Drop steel bars around my gladness
I wont know it
O drop steel bars around my gladness
I wont know it

WE SHALL BOAST ANYWAY:
LIKE LOVE I SAY.
                W.H. Auden

I want everybody to know I am a writer
I will write you a poem
O turn off the latest news bulletins
I dont want to hear them
Turn me over to the cops
I'll surrender
O turn me over to the cops
I surrender

1-513-861 9673
100 Clinton Springs
Cincinnati, Ohio
45217

Dear Editor:

Have been trying to get these poems out for two weeks, but my
censor will not let anything get through-- she's my wife. I
mean she objects to my letters, which I entend to entertain.
While I am not going to let her see this, I shall consider her
point and try to not say something that will turn you against
the poems; and I just might have done it already, but no matter
mind it; I wont, because I have been trying to get into Poetry
magazine since the days of Carl Shapiro,- he said it took him
2 years to get in. Henry Rago encouraged both my letters and
my poems, but didn't except any.

I have had poems in THE NAKED EAR, YUGEN, PROFILE, THE WEST END
HORIZONS and THE INDEPENDENT EYE. My wife is writing , also.
To keep things hormonious, I have suggested she send some to
POETRY magazine, because I know you wont print her stuff as
you wont print mine; and that way I can still tell her I am
a misunderstood poet, and she is also. If I told her where
she can get her poems published, she would do so and then
she might think she is better than I am. As far as I am
concerned, there is only one magazine for first rate poetry,
which I think is what you look for. POETRY! POETRY!

I think language is fun; life should be fun; and poetry is the
link between life and language. Sometimes we lie about lang,
mainly because we dont have it right where we want it; but
the poetry is legitamate if you make clear you are fumbling
when you try to catch it. Sooner or later you have to catch it.
Catch it or die. I caught it in a book size compound of poems
which I call The Seasons. It has one poem for every day of each
of the seasons. I wrote one poem a night for the SEASONS. The h
job is now at hand (hands?), XX XXX XXXand it will take five ye
to polish them.                Sincerly,

# CONVERSATIONS

**Family Memories: Katherine Jones (nee Postell)**
*2023-03-06 to 2024-01-08*
Field Recordings: Michael C. Peterson

*Katherine Postell Jones, 97, is the older sister of Tom Postell and his only surviving immediate family member. Born in Cincinnati on June 25th, 1926, Ms. Jones has been an indispensable source of the family's history. She served as Tom's "tether" to Cincinnati during his darkest final years in New York City. The following is compiled from many hours of recorded visits and transcribed interviews, though countless hours of informal visits and family time have informed the spirit of the conversation. All of the below is taken verbatim from conversations with Miss Kat, as she is affectionately known. Locations and dates have been fact-checked against census data, NPRC records, VA records, court documentation, archival city data, and secondary sources. Despite best efforts to affix precise dates to Postell's movements, much of his time is "lost." For instance, we can potentially trace his hospitalization to one widely-covered, lethal alcohol-related houseparty in Manhattan in 1964 or 1965 but no definitive confirmation can be made. While Katherine was Tom's closest sister, even she did not see him frequently in these years. —Eds.*

Our mother Maud came from a large family from Buford, Georgia and our daddy Thomas Postell Sr. came from a large family from Henderson, Kentucky. He was smart and handsome. Looked Caucasian. A good looker with pretty hair he used to brush fast with two palm brushes. He was a Pullman Porter. He'd be gone ten or fifteen days to places as far away as Salt Lake City. But that's how he got sick. He wouldn't wear long underwear and they got cold on those trains so he ended up in the tuberculosis hospital when he was still young. We were alone a lot because our father was working the railroads and, later, in the hospital.

But when he was home our father liked to play the banjo and the house was full of music. My brother Tee liked to play by himself. He'd mess around. If I asked him to play with his wooden horse, he'd have a little fit. He was quiet. He played in the fireplace and caught on fire once, but it didn't seem to hurt him. We'd have pillow fights, but we didn't get along. I was the oldest—he was 11 months younger than me. Tee was smart and very sensitive. We didn't work as kids—we went to school. We would go swimming at the local pools and went to a lot of movie theaters. We loved the movies. They were our life, our heart. Mama's two sisters, Maggie and Elise, were ticket girls at the Regal. Aunt Maggie taught me how to work the food counter, selling bottles of pop and hot dogs. Tee loved cowboy movies and we'd get in for free—the aunts would split a ticket in half for us. Our dad and our uncles were great ball players, but Tee didn't care for playing baseball. He went to the movies and wrote a lot.

We really missed having a father. He was a good man—everybody liked him. We discovered that he was becoming a good painter while he was in the hospital. Dunham was full. That was in Mid Price Hill. Back off the road. It was a huge hospital. People were dying right and left even after two or three doses. It was the three of us kids—me and Tee and Pauline—and we were young. We couldn't work or nothing. Dad was in his thirties—so he was young too. He lived nine years in Dunham. People were bringing food to put in his closet. We had a horrible life. My mom caught hell—she didn't catch heck—she caught *hell* without him. We had the Maxeys (my mother's parents) who helped and they got us moved together in a building on 4th Street called the San Rafael building. It had eight stories and my grandmother's kids Elise and her husband Dan, and Uncle Jake got an apartment in the San Rafael—apartment #37 on the eighth floor—and different folks moved in. They had six bedrooms and a lobby with a piano that Aunt Elise wound up giving me (but I couldn't pay to haul it). It was a beautiful black player piano. There wasn't a scratch on it.

Tee was always working then and he had a big desk. He went to high school up to the 11th grade. Then he got mad at a teacher. Well, a teacher got mad at him. And so he went off to the Navy. He went out West to California and then Hawaii during the end of the second war. The first time, he served as a gunner's mate, first class, in Hawaii. And then when he went back into the Navy the second time, he was an officer. He transported troops. That's what they called it, "transporting troops." And he did well in the Navy. I don't think it had to be that . . . because we were light, but we were considered colored. He came back, finished high school, and then he went to college. Then he went on to Chase Law at Northern Kentucky University to be a lawyer; he went for several years, but didn't finish.

Our daddy died after nine years in hospital. They thought our mother had mental illness; she was just upset because of losing our dad and was having such a hard time. She was grieving, but Tee stayed a long time and helped her. We all helped her but Tee lived with Mom in what we called the Laurel Homes—320 Laurel. I lived in another apartment because I was married, in downtown Cincinnati, the West End. I lived at 1330 Baymiller on the corner of Lincoln Park Drive (now we call it Ezzard Charles) and Bay Mill, right on the corner on the third floor. And Mama lived in a home where Tee took care of her for a while. Our sister Pauline had gone away to college when Tee went (for the first time) into the Navy. The second time he enlisted, however, he'd just fallen out with her. Pauline wanted my mama to stay with some lady friends so she gave away Tee's furniture (he had bought a lot of furniture for his and our mother's apartment). Tee came home one day and Pauline was giving it away to make mama move in with a friend, Miss Annie Frank Allen. He got really upset and left—went to New York. They had a nice apartment and he had a drumkit there.

He came home from the Navy the first time with those drums. He was a good drummer and fast. He'd play these— what do you call them—rimshots? Hard and fast loud smacks. He loved the rimshots. Drove us all crazy. He and Snooky Gibson were best friends: they were musicians together and had a band. Snooky owned the barbershop on Reading Road and it was popular among both whites and blacks. Later, the mayor—one or two mayors, really—destroyed it. It had a lot of customers. Snooky had brothers that everybody knew and liked. They were well-liked, the Gibson brothers, just like the Postells. A lot of folks went to Snooky's: to play music, to just be together, to hang out. Wilbert Longmire was Tee's good friend. He'd always come through. But really you'd never know who'd show up—talented guys just come in and start harmonizing. And Tee was likable—he got along with everybody. Good sense of humor, real easy going. But no one knew he wrote poems. I didn't either.

After Tee had left, I went to New York and stayed in New York, Long Island, and Elizabeth and New Jersey. I was a nurse. I went up to New York for a common job but I didn't get a college education. So when I showed up I was living with a lady. Took me to see Tee. He was on the third floor of a building on Ninth Street but he wouldn't have no company. He lived on Sixth Street too at some point. Originally I was going to Philadelphia where my daddy's sister was. I was on my way to leave Cincinnati, on my way to see our Aunt Pauline—in Philadelphia—when a family friend named Marie O'Hare called and told me to come on up there. She was my daddy's friend and she had family here in Cincinnati but had moved to New Jersey and had bought an old furnished house on 60 Jewett Avenue in Jersey City. I could stay upstairs. Tee was in New York City by that time, but my maid job was on Long Island. I stayed up there a few months and took care of three little kids. I was supposed to visit Tee and at one point Marie took me over to find him on North Street somewhere. We didn't go up to his apartment but later he came down—he didn't want us to see his place. He said he had to clean up because he was always working and jumping around—had a lot of papers and junk around. He had a good artist friend there by the name of LeRoi Jones.

So me and Marie did go to see him but he told us to come back later. Marie said "hell, it's cold out here," so we went on home. But we did go back. We ended up sending him home. He got sick. He'd gone to a party and everybody got real sick from the drinking—they'd cut the alcohol with something and he had to go to the hospital. I heard that thirty-seven people died from drink that night he was hospitalized, if I recall. I remember Bellevue—they saved Tee. He stayed in the hospital for awhile. Something wasn't right. I went and got him and he wouldn't come with me and Marie. He was proud—didn't want to stay in New Jersey. He wanted to stay in New York. He went back over to his place but the landlord had taken all his paper. All of his writings were gone. All his belongings were gone. Landlord, probably, because he was in the hospital for so long. That's how a lot of his stuff got left, too. He had lost all his typewritten stuff when he was in the hospital.

From that point he had a hard time. It was terrible. I had a part-time job that wasn't enough to support him in another apartment. I was sorry about that. He lived here and there for a long time. He was homeless—had to pay every day. Shelters, weekly hotels. Maybe friends' places. So I got my husband Jeff Bond up there. He came over there, we got an apartment and we tried to get him to stay over in New Jersey with Jeff. I was staying on at another job at that time as a housekeeper and nurse taking care of Miss Evelyn Bailey, a teacher. She and her husband and brother had a house in Elizabeth, New Jersey. I was staying with them and coming home on the weekend, Thursdays or Fridays. Jeff couldn't stay with me so we had to find Jeff a place to stay in Elizabeth. I found him a room that had a sink, refrigerator, stove, and a big bed. We tried to get Tee to stay with Jeff but he wouldn't do that. He preferred New York. He didn't want New Jersey. He was in bad shape by that point. So we got him, took him to a bar, got him high drinking, and got him on a bus. But the bus was to Cincinnati. He thought he was on a bus uptown but he was so high he didn't know. And Pauline got him at the bus station. She told us to send him home, she'd get him. He was upset but I wasn't there to hear it.

We didn't want him to get hurt. We didn't want him to go hungry. We wanted to take care of him. He was our only brother and our family *always* stuck together. He was lucky. I always prayed for him. When he came home he went right into the Longview alcoholic ward. That's where he met Rose.

**Rose Bianchi: A Conversation**
Finneytown, Cincinnati
*2023-05-21*
Anthony Sutton & Michael C. Peterson, interviewers

*Rose Bianchi was married to Tom Postell from 1971 until his death in 1980. Bianchi first met Postell in Cincinnati's Longview Hospital in 1970. Since Bianchi's first solicitation for help with Postell's typescripts in 2020, countless conversations, both recorded and informal, have taken place. She is the primary linkage to Postell's manuscripts* Poems from the Tomb *and* Seasons, *along with his contributor copies of* Yugen *and* The Naked Ear. *Tom's original "green book"—a one-off, professionally bound volume of Tom's favorite poems presumably gifted to him by a local friend sometime in 1971–72—has not been locatable. Bianchi endured significant grief upon learning of Tom's death in June of 1980 while on a family trip to Pennsylvania. Many of Tom's personal belongings (with the exception of poetry-related items) were disposed of soon after his passing. She continues to live in Cincinnati, Ohio. —Eds.*

**Editors:** You've mentioned that you first met Tom at Longview State Hospital in 1970, after he returned to Cincinnati from New York City. How did you first come to know each other and what were your first impressions of him?

**Rose Bianchi:** Well, I was employed at Longview as a music therapist. Actually, I was a music teacher, but they called me a "music therapist." I worked in the activities department, which was a different place in the hospital from the wards themselves. The patients could sign up for art or music or library use. And only certain patients at Longview were free to come to these meetings. Tee was one of them. He had checked himself in for alcohol abuse disorder. I had a group of about maybe seven or eight men and women who came to the room where I worked and basically just listened to music. I came to know Tee when he began to request jazz recordings and some classical recordings. I realized that he knew a lot about music—in some instances more than I did—so I was very impressed with his knowledge, and also with his demeanor. He was always rather quiet and focused and didn't have a lot to say, but when he did say something it seemed to be worth listening to. This went on for several months. Then at one point Tee handed me a sheaf of papers—a sheaf of his poems—and he said, "This is who I am." I took those poems home and read them. I guess I had been gradually falling in love with Tee all along. After I read his poetry I fell in love with the poems.

**Eds:** What was your impression of the poems when you read them?

**RB:** I thought they were beautiful and they affected me—even though often I didn't understand the poems. But whether I understood them or not, I felt them. And I loved them. He only gave me a few poems. But then gradually he persuaded somebody at Longview to put together a book of his poetry, which was that green book, *Poems from the Tomb*. So, really, I fell in love with the poems.

**Eds:** It sounds like he really announced himself as a poet to you?

**RB:** Yes, he did. And he thought of himself as a poet. I mean, he said, *this is who I am.* So I understood that in loving the poems, I had to love the poet.

**Eds:** *Poems from the Tomb* was written prior to you encountering each other.

**RB:** Yes, uh-huh.

**Eds:** That said, was that the first work he invited you into?

**RB:** Yes, that was the first work he shared. Well, before that, he gave me a couple of pages. And the pages were, I think, his best poems. The one about Gertrude Stein, the one about Billie Holiday. There were only three or four poems in the first set that he gave me.

**Eds:** "I Want a Solid Piece of Sunlight"?

**RB:** "And a Yardstick to Measure It With." Yes.

**Eds:** How did—when he spoke about that book, or he mentioned those poems, how did he—

**RB:** No, he didn't. Not once. He didn't speak of that book or those poems.

**Eds:** He didn't even speak about his feelings for them or about their composition?

**RB:** He never did. He just never talked like that.

**Eds:** Did he speak much about his time living in New York City or his friendship with Amiri Baraka or other poets?

**RB:** He talked very, very little about New York. At one point he said he would love to take me to New York where I could experience some of those bars in Greenwich Village where he had heard so much good music, but we never did go to New York. We did go to Chicago together and heard some good jazz there. But he didn't talk about New York. He talked very little about anything actually. He was quiet. So quiet. I only learned about his experience in New York through his poetry. He seemed to have a kind of a love-hate relationship with LeRoi Jones. That was my impression. Maybe: admiration and disapprobation would be better words.

**Eds:** You married each other in 1971. What was your life together like? How did his writing process sit in your life together?

**RB:** Well, he didn't write at the beginning of our life together. He was recently discharged from Longview. He still had meetings with his psychiatrist. She came to our apartment several times. He was taking a lot of medication, and the medication made him very sleepy. He went to barbering school at one time. His good friend, Donald

"Snooky" Gibson, was a barber. I suppose because of that he thought perhaps he could succeed as a barber too—but that never panned out. He kind of quit halfway through. I was teaching school and pretty busy teaching full-time. And he was staying at home, working, and listening to music. Doing whatever he did during the day. At some point he started going over to Snooky's barbershop and hung out for a couple hours every afternoon, just to talk with people. About jazz mostly, I think. He spent one year in AA, and during that year, for some reason, at the beginning of the year, an acquaintance of ours suggested that he write a poem a day, and that's when he started working on what became *The Seasons*. And he would write a poem at night, actually. I would go to bed, and he would start writing his poem. And when I got up in the morning, there was a new poem at the breakfast table, which was awfully exciting to me. That was an ongoing thing; that went on for a year.

**Eds:** He had stopped drinking that year?

**RB:** He stopped drinking for a couple months after Longview and started again. He went to AA for that year in 1975 and he stopped drinking briefly. But he was also pretty heavily medicated. Another story he told about his beginning drinking was that he was so cold that he drank to keep warm. But this was as an adult. Maybe in New York City. That's how he really started drinking. I don't remember all the ramifications of that story. But the basis was that he drank liquor to stay warm, and that's what started its all. I think he drank some pretty awful stuff before we got together. And, you know, as I look back, his life was so inextricably tied to alcohol that I can't imagine his life without it. I think he needed it—or *he* thought he needed it.

**Eds:** What was the rhythm of your household like on a typical day back then?

**RB:** Well, if it was a weekday, I would get up early and go to work. And when I came home, Tee would take off for a couple of hours and go over to Snooky's. And then we would have dinner and usually listen to music or watch some television. On the weekends, we usually went out and we would go to the Cincinnati Public Library or we would go to a record store and buy some music and take it home and listen to it. We would go out to dinner quite often on the weekends. When we went to the library, I usually went to the classical music section and looked at recordings. And Tee usually went to the poetry section and read through journals to see what was going on in poetry. It was there that he discovered the poem that Amiri Baraka wrote to Tom Postell, a dead black poet. He was pretty excited when he discovered that poem and I couldn't figure out why because I thought it was pretty insulting.

**Eds:** Could you tell us about that moment when he read that poem?

**RB:** He came running over to where I was and said, "look at this." I looked at it and, well, we were both impressed that Baraka wrote a poem about Tee. I thought that it was rather a bittersweet moment because the poem really wasn't anything magnificent. I'm not sure it was in praise of his poetry, although maybe it was.

**Eds:** What other library materials did he like to check out?

**RB:** He didn't really do much reading when we were together. He said that he had already read everything worth reading.

But he did suggest books for me to read. He suggested I read Rimbaud's *Illuminations*. He loved French poets. He loved Verlaine, Rimbaud, and Baudelaire. I was working on a PhD in music history and I needed to take fifteen credits unrelated to my major. So I decided to take literature and philosophy. He suggested that I use my fifteen credits to learn about James Joyce. So that's when I was introduced to Joyce. I never got to *Finnegan's Wake*, but I did learn to love his other work.

**Eds:** His sister Katherine mentioned that he was quite an aspiring jazz drummer. What was the role of music in your life together?

**RB:** There was always music in our house, *always*. Either jazz or classical music. One of the things we loved most was going out and picking out recordings, reading record jackets, and going home and getting high and listening to music. So that was mainly what we did with music. We did have a piano. I played the piano quite often. He didn't comment on that very much, so I don't know if he enjoyed it or not [laughs]. He seemed to idolize jazz musicians. I remember one day he picked me up after work and he had tears in his eyes. He said that Charles Mingus had died that day. And he was very, very troubled by that. I could never hear the bass in those jazz recordings. So I didn't really appreciate Charles Mingus because my hearing wasn't that great that I could pick it out. He also loved Thelonius Monk. He introduced me to Art Tatum too. Fell in love with Tatum.

**Eds:** A couple of the poems, like "I Was Once a Sober Fox," sort of overtly address this sense of invisibility he seemed to feel. That seemed to be a weight he carried with him . . .

**RB:** Yes. (Citing Postell) "I was born on Pike's Peak and if my parents noticed, they didn't raise any hell about it."

**Eds:** They seem to address a sense of invisibility in the higher vaults of the literary or art worlds. The voice on the page, though—it can be a raucous voice.

**RB:** Yeah, in some of those poems, like going out to the ballpark or watching a movie. "Go out to the ballpark and watch me get batted around" or something like that. Right. That's pretty vigorous.

**Eds:** Some real self-effacing stuff in there, but the voices, as you're saying, almost visibly vivid. What was the word you used?

**RB:** Vigorous.

**Eds:** Vigorous. That's a great word for it. As far as you could tell, from where did this feeling stem?

**RB:** I just think that anybody as brilliant as Tee, who had to grow up in this society, I don't know how anyone as sensitive and brilliant as Tee could grow up in this society without being damaged by it.

**Eds:** Did he have a community here—or writers with whom he could share his work?

**RB:** No, he didn't. He didn't have any community apart from occasionally we visited his relatives and his fellowship with the guys at the barbershop. His idea of marriage was complete togetherness, which did not sit well with me. So he didn't really have friends of his own except for Snooky Gibson and those associations.

**Eds:** It's interesting to think about your family backgrounds. You came from a pretty large Italian family in Pennsylvania. Tee came from an African-American family, similarly large, with roots in Kentucky and Ohio, and even further back in Georgia. How did Cincinnati treat an interracial couple like yourselves in 1971?

**RB:** We didn't—the only kind of prejudice we experienced was when Tee was discharged from Longview and before we got married, we lived together in the apartment that I had on Eden Avenue, and we were evicted from that apartment. I was evicted because the landlord didn't like "the company I was keeping." So Tee said that since we didn't have any money we couldn't really fight it, and so we were evicted. So that was one thing that happened. The other thing that happened was when we were in the library one time, a man kind of made a pass at me, and I ignored him and walked over to the table where Tee was sitting, and the man then yelled—he yelled at me using the N-word. And Tee went up to an officer who was there at the library and said he wanted to press charges because someone was making offensive language towards his wife. But those were the only two instances of blatant problems that we had.

**Eds:** Aside from your experiences, did you sense that this was the culture of the city at that time?

**RB:** I was pretty clueless, actually. As I said, we were pretty much enmeshed with each other. Didn't have a—didn't have a big range of friendship or even family. And so I don't really know what it was like.

**Eds:** As a Californian transplant to Cincinnati, I find it to be a hybrid place: semi-urbanized and semi-rural. There's a strong working class history but with pockets of immense wealth. Historically, it's a north-south border town straddling this diagonally-running, working river. What was the city like in the 60's and 70's?

**RB:** I thought it was extremely conservative. I mean, well—it is conservative. I didn't like Cincinnati at all when I first came. So after about five years, I stopped cheering for the Pirates and started cheering for the Reds. And I—I still kind of feel like a transplant to Cincinnati.

**Eds:** I know you lived at 100 Clinton Springs in North Avondale. That historically was one of the first areas of the city where Black homeownership was tenable. One of the first mixed neighborhoods of the city. What was your experience living at Clinton Springs like? I assume this was after you moved from Eden Avenue?

**RB:** After we moved from Eden Avenue, we moved to a place in Mount Auburn and then we moved to Clinton Springs. Yeah, it was fun.

**Eds:** Did Tom have similar feelings about Cincinnati or do you have a sense of what his feelings on the city were?

**RB:** Uh, no. I don't know if he felt that way or not. I know he loved baseball.

**Eds:** But did the city find its way into his work?

**RB:** I have the impression that it had to since it was so much a part of him and his family. But I don't think of him as a Cincinnati poet or an Ohio poet. I think of him as a New York poet. His poetry seems to be linked more to New York than it does to Cincinnati. It seems more—I don't know—global. His imagination just seemed unlocked in that period. I think New York was kind of a salvation for him. I mean, he got to associate with other poets and musicians and be part of the beat generation. It must have been a godsend for him to be among people who, I want to say, understood him, maybe understood him as an artist, although maybe didn't get personally involved with him.

**Eds:** Do you see race as an issue crucial to Tom and his work? And to yourselves?

**RB:** Yes, definitely. To his life. I think that living in this racist society was the reason for his emotional and mental problems. And I think those problems came out in his poetry. I just think that the kind of treatment that African-Americans receive in society today is bad enough, let alone back then. I always assumed with Tee it was related to growing up in a racist society, because he was a brilliant person: extremely sensitive, very talented, an introvert. We didn't argue about race. We did have arguments about homophobia, because I couldn't understand why he felt the way he did. He was homophobic, and I think in a way he was afraid of gay men. I don't know what went on in New York, but his attitude towards gay men seemed to stem from his time in New York.

**Eds:** In *Seasons*, he writes:

> I'm a black man, and I know there are plenty white poets saying things that need be said. That is there were white poets. All of them have died, and the extant white poets are extraneous, bubbling and bubbling and bubbling and bubbling and bubbling and bubbling and bubbling.

He goes on, and he says, "I like Gary Snyder, but with an Amiri Baraka splicing words together, I don't like Gary Snyder."

**RB:** I think there's a lot of bitterness and anger in *The Seasons*—and frustration.

**Eds:** There are wonderful images of solitude in his work, both in *Tomb* and *Seasons*. He writes:

> I grow crops in a desert near an oasis of rum.
> My plants are a mirage.
> People run to them and die . . . .
> I am not a mirage, though I gather their bones for fuel.
> It's funny that black or white, the bones are all the same color.
> I'll keep doing this till I see some sign or hear some voice.
> Come out of the sky, a comet or a funnel cloud coming right at me.
> I guess I'm dead for a while.
> I just wanted to say so long and wish you all well while I am away.

It's hard not to think of *Tomb* here. So many elegies and self-elegies in this book. "Charlie Parker Died," for instance, which are elegies about figures of importance to him. But then in "Seems Silly to Quibble," he writes, "Let us go into sleep and dream in the dark saliva of God. / Fought gained lost the trial and loved lost and won the deal and died." Did you get a sense that Tom gravitated towards death as an ideal state or outcome?

**RB:** Yes, I think. I think he attempted suicide a couple of times before I met him. And I think that he committed himself to Longview because he had recently attempted suicide—like he had just kind of thrown himself in the middle of a street. I think it was like a shadow that always followed him. And I think he was always in solitude, even when he was with other people. There was sort of like a cloud of solitude around him. He didn't believe in small talk at all. He didn't believe in saying anything unless you had something to say that was worth listening to. That makes for a lot of solitude. And so this cloud of solitude and the shadow of death were always with him. I think he was just a very, very sick man.

**Eds:** His few successes were for him great successes. But we've talked a little bit about his departure from New York, his not being in the scene anymore, as perhaps a liability to him in some ways. There seems to be a real compulsion in him to keep going.

**RB:** And yet he couldn't write. I sometimes get the feeling that when we were together he only spent that one year writing. It often seemed like he needed to write but couldn't write. And, you know, speaking of oases, I think that his time in New York was a brief oasis in his life. He came alive when he was in New York. He was writing and he was associating with writers and musicians. Then that was over and he became incapacitated. He only came alive when we would go to the library and he would go and read the poetry magazines. There would be a spark of life in him, as though he felt like maybe he could re-enter that scene again. But it didn't happen.

**Eds:** One of the first things that you mentioned when I met you that I'm curious about is that you and Tom had at one point taken French classes.

**RB:** Yes. I believe at the University of Cincinnati. It was a night class.

**Eds:** Could you talk a bit more about that?

**RB:** Well, he didn't seem to enjoy the class as much as I did. He thought the professor was trying to get too close to me. It was completely off base there. It was completely imaginary. Nothing like that was happening. So this was not a successful time.

**Eds:** Did he speak any other languages or try his hand at translating?

**RB:** No, he was only interested in French. I can't remember either of us working on translating.

**Eds:** I know that you had reached out to Amiri Baraka. And one can find a letter, your letter, to Baraka in the archive at Columbia.

**RB:** Yeah, it took him three years to answer me. He sent me a postcard and suggested I send Tee's poems to *Poetry Magazine* and what was the other periodical, *Paris Review*? As if Tee hadn't already done that, you know. He'd sent poems to

*Poetry Magazine.* He was especially excited when he got a pink rejection slip because that was the highest color of a rejection slip you could get, he told me.

**Eds:** Did he submit to other places that you knew of?

**RB:** No, I don't remember that he submitted anywhere else. He didn't. I don't even know what he sent in.

**Eds:** This reminds us—was he a postal carrier for a while?

**RB:** He wasn't a carrier. He worked at night and I don't know what they did at night. That was when we were together. He worked there for about six months.

**Eds:** His sister Katherine mentioned to me that he had done a stint in law school.

**RB:** Oh, that's right. I'd forgotten about that. He had done . . . . He had tried to put himself through law school. He didn't talk about that at all.

**Eds:** Why do you think he wanted to become a lawyer?

**RB:** I have no idea. Maybe he wanted to correct some of the ills of society.

**Eds:** Does law strike you as a natural fit for Tom?

**RB:** No.

**Eds:** You don't think he would have been a good lawyer?

**RB:** He never talked! I mean, how could he be a good lawyer when he never talked? Rarely. Like at home, out in the world, he was just very, very quiet. I remember not long after we were married, I was making conversation at breakfast because it was so quiet. And he said, "You don't have to make up conversation." And I was thinking, well, if I had wanted to sit here alone, why would I get married? But I didn't say it.

**Eds:** In your experience with the poems as you've read them, as you've seen them, as we've spent time with them over these last years—what do you think Tom wanted his readers to experience when reading his work?

**RB:** I think he would want his readers to see him as he really was, to appreciate his intellect, his artistry, his talent, his person. He wanted to be seen and appreciated for who he was, I think.

**Eds:** So much of the feeling in these poems follows from his being a sensitive person—a person of deep interior—injured by the world.

**RB:** Well, American society is a dangerous place for African Americans—it would be hard for an African American to grow up in this society without being profoundly affected by that violence and prejudice. And I have a feeling that he was deeply scarred by a prejudice that was even worse back then than it is now. I mean, he was born in 1927, so he was growing up in the 30s and 40s. I think that's a good reason. Life must have been a lot more dangerous and a lot more, well, terrible for African Americans then than it is even now. Someone who is extremely sensitive and talented and intelligent would find that extremely difficult to put up with, I would imagine. I think Tee was deeply traumatized by it. I think it was the source of all his problems.

**Eds:** In his poem, "Charlie Parker in Bohemia," he writes:

> We owls watch quietly and fill up our bags with these secrets
> and wait patiently till we are overburdened.
> And then we move through the sky like gentlemen
> when day has foreclosed . . . .

These lines strike me as interesting, given what you just said. That feels like a quintessentially Tom line. He turns us into these wise owls who should know better, overburdened with a wisdom that comes from a world writ large.

**RB:** And then what do they do with this wisdom?

**Eds:** Not sure. Tom writes that we move through the sky like gentlemen, but the day has foreclosed. How did Tom move through this overburdening as you saw it?

**RB:** I think he was struck down by it.

# LINER NOTES

# A SHADOW SHOCKED IN MORPHINE: VISIONS OF ARTHUR RIMBAUD IN *POEMS FROM THE TOMB*

## Anthony Sutton

In the NYC Lower East Side during the 50's and 60's, one could go to open mic nights at coffee shops Les Deux Megots (not to be confused with the one in Paris where James Baldwin would write) and Le Metro to see young poets Frank O'Hara, Allen Ginsberg, and Amiri Baraka read their works. In *All Poets Welcome: The Lower East Side Poetry Scene in the 1960's* by Daniel Kane, one can further learn how substantial an influence this moment was for U.S. poetry:

> Poets associated with Les Deux Megots and Le Metro often looked to and discussed earlier alternative literary movements that prompted oral presentation and typographical innovation, thus situating themselves within a literary genealogy. Influenced by their reading and

recuperation of earlier Avant-Garde experimental work, including Italian and Russian futurism, dada, and the texts of radical modernist figures, many writers at the coffee shops highlighted the poem as a spoken phenomenon and typed or "scored" their writing to emphasize its place on both page and stage" (12).

This generation of poets later formed literary schools including the New York School, the Beats, Black Mountain College, and the Black Arts Movement. In addition to importing the experiments thriving throughout Europe they thoroughly integrated new-to-them technologies, for instance the typewriter and the "field poetics" of Charles Olsen, which made explicit the blank page's possibilities. By this time, Tom Postell had long been a resident of Greenwich Village, having fled his hometown of Cincinnati after a family dispute.

The degree to which Postell participated in this scene while living in New York City remains untraceable, lost in the haze of rowdy nights. However, many of the aesthetic virtues and genealogies of this "alternative literary scene" flow through Postell's work. One of his most typographical poems, "[There they sit vacantly      the]" requires two readers to speak simultaneously. At the same time, Postell's work offers a racial critique of New York City's alternative poetry. In *Poems from the Tomb* the visual field of a page serves as score to the jazz-infused poetics reminiscent of Langston Hughes. The blurring between this alternative poetics and yet other racial alternatives makes Postell's work a dynamic contribution to U.S. letters. The music Postell scored bridges the sensibilities of African American poetry and the Western European Avant-Garde, providing a slew of unlikely influences.

From Amiri Baraka's *Autobiography*, we get some snippets of the Tom Postell who wandered the streets of New York. As Baraka describes him:

> [H]e'd been influenced by surrealists of one kind or another, and he was kind of wiggy anyway . . . he was a *real* poet. He had a sureness to his hand . . . that came from practice and knowing what he wanted to say (135).

However, Baraka adds a difficulty by attributing this description to a man named Tim Poston. We know from scholar Aldon Lynn Nielsen that because Baraka's *Autobiography* "often employs both pseudonyms and real names for the same individuals . . . I suspect that his 'Tim Postin' and 'Tom Postell' are both Tom Postell" (81). Additionally, the conversation with Rose Bianchi in this volume reveals that Postell wrote poetry to express the wondrous and ambitious mind behind the wiggyness. Poems like "I Want a Solid Piece of Sunlight and a Yardstick to Measure it With" show how sharply Tom could handle imagery while unabashedly eager to speak nonsense. Because each line of this poem is a sentence, the poem suggests the style of the flaneur: lonely, constant wandering.

We also know from Rose that "surrealists of one kind or another," James Joyce, Gertrude Stein, Charles Baudelaire, and Arthur Rimbaud, were central to Tom Postell's poetics. The last of these figures is named explicitly in the poem "The Rabbit was Rimbaud." Despite the cacophonous influences Postell brings together, this essay focuses on Rimbaud shocked in morphine (to quote the first line of *Poems from the Tomb*). I do this, in part, because I believe the aesthetic principles of French Romanticism allowed Postell to turn his troubles into art. Postell believed living in a state of drunkenness made life new and exciting, an idea that appears in Baudelaire's essay "The Painter of Modern Life." Moreso, Baudelaire's and Rimbaud's embrace of darkness (with books titled *Flowers of Evil* and *A Season in Hell*) as an aesthetic resonates with the apocalyptic visions found in Postell's writing. Visions also put Postell more in line with Rimbaud than Baudelaire: Postell is not chronicling the urban life of New York City but peers into the other world behind it. This essay conjures the spirit of Rimbaud wandering through *Poems from the Tomb* to reveal how Postell turned influence into invention.

I propose Postell's poem "Moon Rocks for Mother" is his rendition of Rimbaud's titular poem "A Season in Hell." Both begin as dramatic monologue: Rimbaud's speaker recalls the memory of turning his soul over to evil while Postell begins with the more narrative act of chopping moon rocks in order to bury them into the earth. "Moon Rocks for Mother" does not detail a descent, but rather the speaker begins to experience paranoia about putting rocks into the hole they dug, claiming it all looks to be "falling like Christ / on our loved ones." The speaker moves on to wreak havoc on earth, thinking of a woman until the speaker gets hung upside down on a weeping willow, only to run after her with the willow and noose dangling around his neck. All this happens while there are "birds splashing up from hell," their chirps echoing from Rimbaud's poem.

Other echoes from "A Season in Hell" reverberate through "Moon Rocks for Mother." Wine is of great importance to both speakers. For Rimbaud's speaker "all wines flowed" before giving their soul over to Satanic forces. Postell's speaker drinks several great wines and begins crank-calling:

> I drank great wines and dialed long distance operators all
> over the world.

I told them I am a black man and I just zipped down the
seams of my soul.
I hung up before they could answer, except for Copenhagen, I
heard no answer from Copenhagen: they said Kierkegaard
was dead now.
For long days, I sat with tongue in cheek watching
television, watching laughter.

This moment echoes the act of addressing Satan that ends
"A Season in Hell." Rimbaud's speaker invokes Satan and
rips out pages from his notebook of the damned in order
to hand over the act of writing. For Rimbaud's speaker,
giving up writing, which may be the same as giving up
their soul, is a way of diverting responsibility. If idle hands
are the devil's playthings, this speaker is giving Satan
pen and paper to write with, too. Postell's speaker also
diverts, but this diversion ends up in absurdity. In spite
of the speaker's hanging up before anyone can answer,
he receives information from Copenhagen instead (even
though the speaker, curiously, claimed they didn't hear
anything). In the next line the reader sees the emptiness in
the speaker's life. The resonance between the nineteenth and
20th centuries falls apart. In one century, giving oneself up
to frivolousness is to descend to hell and in the next century
such frivolousness is merely domestic.

Part of Tom's homage is his grappling with the stakes of
A Season in Hell in order to raise them. The mark that begins
the descent of Rimbaud's speaker is the act of "pulling Beauty
down on my knees" (264). Postell's speaker mirrors this by
bringing down all of 19th century French poetry:

I dug a hole to drop the rocks, and posed, rocks in hands,
dropping them,

divorcing them, one by one, like I did the nineteenth
century French poets,
    freeing them, dropping them.

There is a playful recursivity to how Postell puts Rimbaud and his cohort in the position Rimbaud put Beauty in. At the same time, Rimbaud is like Postell's rocks: abandoned, not too different from how Rimbaud's speaker "was able to expel from my mind all human hope." In a deviation from Rimbaud, Postell ends "Moon Rocks for Mother" with more irresponsible behavior as the speaker plays a prank on a woman by telling her "the ocean was to blame." For what exactly is unclear, though the speaker mockingly follows with "And she believed me." The poem's final line, an italicized *Plop* suggests that Postell's speaker ends in a more ironic place than Rimbaud's. Postell's speaker may have found that the joke was on him, perhaps the ocean *was* to blame, leaving him less Faustus and more boy-who-cried-wolf.

Rimbaud's shadow also emerges in the final poem of *Tomb* we have included in this volume, "WXYZ." In Rimbaud's sonnet "Vowels," his speaker synesthetically draws out colors that correlate with vowels of the alphabet: "A black, E white, I red, U green, O blue" (64). Kenneth Koch, a poet associated with New York and born in Cincinnati a couple years before Tom, described Rimbaud's work as thinking "poetry had a power nothing else had, because poetry could be a way to see beyond reality. He thought that what people called reality was only a surface, and beyond that surface a lot more was going on" (69). In Rimbaud's work, this extends beyond "Vowels" and into his book *Illuminations* which uses the power of associative thinking to generate visionary experiences of the world. A level of insight and imagination that illuminates life, the speakers of *Illuminations* communicate through unpredictable sentences made exciting by how their images run through unconventional syntax.

"WXYZ" shows the illuminated world Postell could see. Unlike Rimbaud, Tom's world does not begin synesthetically, but comes through desperation:

> anything for a poem
> cut wrists
> all things lay down before the poem.

Then blasphemy ignites the poem: "o lord your head is blowing up." As "WXYZ" unravels, it reverberates between registers both silly and violent with lines ending with alliterative phrases such as "chop chop" and "drop dead." Another contrast to "Vowels" is that Tom's world does not have the one-to-one ratio of Rimbaud's. In one line the speaker vows that "for a poem I will give up black white but not green women." While that line seemingly gives a nod to the original *Star Trek* character Vina, a green-skinned Orion woman who is depicted as a sex slave, it also suggests a certain kind of stakes. The lack of punctuation in this line provides a futurist speed and blur. Black and white swirl together in meaninglessness, and the green slave woman from *Star Trek* (and thus, the imagination, the object of desire, desire itself) becomes poetry's most necessary element.

That's not the only place where silliness energizes "WXYZ." In line 15 begins what might first appear as a parody of "Vowels":

> a strung green words and lanterns along love's grove and
>     moved over time
> a stood up and dewigged grew a beard for tomorrow shall
>     be sad
> b lives among green trees with a broken heart

> b will not sing again will not greet spring again or build
>     fire again, either
> b is full of shit as a christmas turkey
> c is happy and swims in a silver puddle of water
> c is a harpy with golden wings.

While for Rimbaud each vowel has a distinct color and flare to bring out, Postell saw multiple personalities in each of the first three letters of the alphabet. Each letter has a distinct affect, performs some kind of action: "a" and "b" have attachments to love, and all these letters are guilty of suspicious behavior.

The strange syntax stretching from each letter suggests not only that Tom's vision is of a messier world than Rimbaud's, but does so in a way that is possible because of Black Englishes in the United States. In June Jordan's essay "Nobody Mean More to Me Than You and the Future Life of Willie Johnson" she describes her teaching of Alice Walker's *The Color Purple* and the student's confusion over the vernacular. Together, Jordan and her students work to perform an English-to-English translation of *The Color Purple*, along the way outlining "rules" of Black English. Their first rule very much applies to Postell's work: "Black English is about a whole lot more than muthafuckin'" (366). For Jordan, Black English's magic depends on it being "incorrect" when compared to "Standard English" and for Rimbaud, magic resides on the other side of language itself. Postell's work contains the synthesis: all language and possibility swirl together into syntactical formulations that couldn't exist anywhere else.

As if to signal as much, Postell closes "WXYZ" by swiftly dismissing the rest of the alphabet, which he says "you can sell on the open market"—a refutation of a poetics firmly grounded in legibility, thus making space for the vivid nonsense characteristic of Postell's poems—followed by the long dash which closes out this iteration of his book, six of them stacked together, reaching out to infinity, or, in other words, us.

# WORKS CITED

Baraka, Amiri. *The Autobiography of LeRoi Jones/Amiri Baraka.* New York City. Freundlich Books. 1984.

Kane, Daniel. *All Poets Welcome: The Lower East Side Poetry Scene in the 1960's.* Berkeley. University of California Press. 2003.

Jordan, June. "Nobody Mean More to Me Than You and the Future Life of Willie Johnson." *Harvard Educational Review.* Vol. 58, No. 3, 1988, pp. 363-374.

Koch, Kenneth and Farrell, Kate. "Arthur Rimbaud." *Sleeping on the Wing: An Anthology of Modern Poetry with Essays on Reading and Writing.* New York City. Vintage Books. 1982.

Nielsen, Aldon Lynn. *Black Chant: Language of African American PostModernism.* Cambridge. University of Cambridge Press. 1997.

Rimbaud, Arthur. *Complete Works, Selected Letters.* Tr. Wallace Fawlie. Chicago. University of Chicago Press. 1966.

Rimbaud, Aruthur. "Vowels." Tr. Kenneth Koch. *Sleeping on the Wing: An Anthology of Modern Poetry with Essays on Reading and Writing.* New York City. Vintage Books. 1982.

# EXHUMED MUSIC

## Derrick Harriell

There's a long list of writers and artists who didn't receive their flowers while they were alive to smell them. There've been volumes of work which graciously remained patient until we, the audience, were finally ready to lend the art its proper consideration. This consideration often did not occur because the art lacked artistic effectiveness, but more so, because we, the audience, were simply not ready to hold the art. This, I believe, is the case with Tom Postell's posthumous poetry collection, *Poems from the Tomb*.

*Poems from the Tomb* is ultimately a macrocosm of music, lyric, and love. These poems are steeped in a very specific Black Arts Movement aesthetic, but the voice is singular in its pursuit of reflective truth. The language moves from very literal to accessible ambiguity. Unexpected image pairings only enhance the world building that occurs. When considering the first few pages it doesn't take long for the reader to gather that we are indeed in a particular world: Postell's world.

The framework of this collection is grounded in music. Poems in which our most celebrated Jazz musicians seem to fall from the sky and decorate this artistic tapestry. Take for example the poem, "Charlie Parker Died." This poem addresses the death of Charlie Parker. It begins as a lament in which our taken musician moves into the afterlife through the reception of our most sacred elements:

> The moon struck dumb
> was high and wailing
> soaking in a sodden
> great black heart. Aloft thru
> the quiet drone of
> the Hero's dream.
>
> Billie Holiday stood before the door of his tomb
> chained to it singing the blues.
> He climbed onto the rooftop among stars drifting light
> and drove his sounds thru the black burning sky.

The imagery of the moon and stars coupled with the mentioning of Billie Holiday creates a surreal-like tone. Our "Hero," Charlie Parker, is moving through a celestial portal all while being ushered by Lady Day (Billie Holiday). These imaginative lyrics highlighting the beginnings of the afterlife brilliantly emphasizes the speaker's reverence for the musician. Furthermore, Holiday functions as a celestial element herself, which is ironic considering that Holiday was still alive when Parker passed away; she too then becomes, a sacred element.

As the poem continues, we can began to wonder if this poem is locked in melancholy. Parker maintains agency throughout and even lays down laws:

> During the resurrection
> he took the barbed wire from the Lord and laid down the
>   law.
> Our pretenses and beliefs were lies and dead."

It seems that the poem is complicating how death might be considered.

> He eschewed it and
> consumed that void. And sadness was torn and beaten
> for wearing baggy pants to church, and from womb to
> womb . . ."

Charlie Parker is mentioned again in the poem "Charlie Parker in Bohemia." This nine-line poem conveys the anticipation of what it's like to almost witness Parker play live. Legend has it that in 1955 a man named Jimmy Garofolo opened a jazz club, Café Bohemia, in Greenwich Village. One night, a patron had one too many Brandy Alexanders and was removed from the club. Said patron was actually Charlie Parker, who lived across the street at the time, and offered to play the club for gratis as a gesture to pay off his debt. Sadly, Parker never had the opportunity to play in Café Bohemia, as he died that same year. The first stanza opens:

> too nonchalant to terrify us
> —presidents trying to prove themselves common place
> sneak off into the night when the security forces are
>   sleeping

and drive recklessly over the backroads of New England
    towns
the souped up automobiles of our desire.

This first stanza creates a mood in which Parker is not only "too nonchalant to terrify us" but also the anticipation of the jazz club is "too nonchalant." Desire functions not only as a compelling emotion in this particular poem but throughout the collection. Here, desire conveys both presidents sneaking off into the night and the crowd's anticipation as they await Parker. The second stanza continues:

we owls watch quietly and fill up our bags
with these secrets and wait patiently til we are overburdened
and then we move through the sky like gentlemen
when day has foreclosed on Charlie Parker in Bohemia.

It's noteworthy here that the crowd is referred to as "owls" given the late hour. The crowd fills up their bags "with these secrets and wait patiently til [they] are overburdened." This final stanza raises several interesting questions: is this a poem in which we imagine Parker actually plays in Café Bohemia, or, does this poem simply comment on Parker as a patron in Café Bohemia. The final line and its emphasis on the foreclosing of the day can be read several ways; does the sun rising foreclose an inconsequential night in which Parker is simply part of the lay audience, or, is the day foreclosing a metaphor referencing Parker's tragic death. Either way, the aforementioned desire awaits within the ethos of the audience.

*Poems from the Tomb* is a body of desire. More than being interested in definitive commentary, these poems pursue productive complications, questionings through the poet's contemplative lens. Among its pursuit of music and finely crafted lyric, love seems to be the most urgent theme. The poet/speaker moves us through the complete kaleidoscope of love, recollection of love, and unrequited love. Poems like "Ann," "Delores," and several poems simply titled "Poem," are reflections of desire and devotion. This noted, the poem "Love Boat" is Postell reaching into all of his literary lyric and love bags. Not only does the poem embody the love theme, but like traditional Blues verse, it employs repetition, and most importantly, it begs. The poem "Love Boat" begins:

> If there are such things as love
> Lift them from my gloom and let them glow
> If there are no such things
> Touch me and hear my song.

The speaker here expresses a sensation of "gloom" and a longing for relief. "Lift them from my gloom and let them glow" is a plea. There's a song inside and longing for that song to be released: a hurt waiting to "glow." "Touch me and hear my song" doubles as both a statement of vulnerability and particular Blues note. Ironically, the speaker doubles as both Blues singer and Blues instrument. This is a fascinating entendre. The Blues being a genre of music in which the guitar produces the melodic heartbeat; here, the speaker is both crooner and heartbeat, both howler and harmony. The second stanza stands firmly in Blues:

> Doooh, here we go, and Tina
> Lifting star bulbs from my brain
> Faaah, thou Tina, lovely Tina
> So, my, me, so my oh my tinatinatina.

This stanza uses repetition and lyric to create urgency and effect. "Doooh" is a song lyric, a note, and the repetition of "tinatinatina," a Blues beg ("baby baby please"). This stanza moves us from the more contemplative first stanza to an illustration of what it means to "hear my song." This song is on full display. Tina is the love interest, and the speaker isn't shy in declaring it: "Tinatinatina." As the poem continues, Tina is constantly summoned and cherished.

> Morning starlight Tina
> Evening starlight Tina
> Limelight Dancelight
> Sweet Georgia Brown
> That's Tina, That's Tina.

A boat image functions as a symbol for the relationship:

> Tina, out of this take me
> Row, row our boat
> Gently through the currents
> Gently
> Listen to me
> We cannot stop.

"Love Boat" is Postell's poetic sensibilities and craft employments on full display. *Poems from the Tomb* is a Black Arts Movement inspired collection. The book is not solely interested in music, lyric, and love; however, these themes sing mightily. There are additional moments in which Postell alludes to canonical writers, nature, and politics. The poet is aware of the pen's power and how it can and should be most effectively deployed. *Poems from the Tomb* takes the reader on a journey and builds a world that the reader can rest in. This world is not always steady, and sometimes the waters can be rough; nonetheless, we are all better off with this art in the world, with the exhuming of these finely crafted poems.

TOM POSTELL

# PICK-UP TRUCKS OF WORDS: AN ANALYSIS OF TOM POSTELL'S "EVEN IF"

## brittny ray crowell

In *The Art of Daring: Risk, Restlessness, Imagination*, Carl Phillips says that "Poetry—the kind that does in fact give us the world as we had not seen it, that makes us question what we had thought we knew . . . is the result of a generative restlessness of imagination" (36). It is in this way that some of my favorite poems are those that are not always immediately accessible to my expectations, but those that exchange my comfort and familiarity for novelty and surprise. While I enjoy a poem that smoothly and easily unfurls, I'm equally fascinated by work that makes my mind stutter and wonder, poems that make me ponder a fresh web of connections, comparisons, and associations. I like to see a poem restless for the thing on the tip of its tongue, to see, as Phillips says, the poet's "obsessions . . . wrestled with" across the page with each image or metaphor that brings us as close as we can to whatever it is they want us to experience (36). Ideally, I like this work to begin with a title that seduces with a little bit of tension, which Tom Postell's poem "Even if" establishes wonderfully. The title instantly ignites my urge to snoop and ear hustle. It's as if I've caught a bit of a conversation passing a doorway leaving me eager to learn what conditions and contexts are to follow ("Even if" *what*? What's going to happen *regardless*?).

Growing up, my grandparents each had their favorite puzzle in the local paper. Grandpa always worked the Jumble while Grandma worked the Cryptoquote. She taught me that the trick was to let the clusters guide you, that the process begins slowly, but once one word was revealed it made it easier to guess what the next word might be, that one uncoded line could be the key to understanding the entire puzzle. Likewise, while "Even if" begins with the hope that we will be made privy to something, the first few lines reveal a tightlipped speaker offering only a series of cryptic statements:

> These Bardic Days churning light upon the loam,
> trundel the sky. So we lie immersed in foam,
> drumming sadness into rocks, and crying lakes. And after
> noon air lifts robins, lifts their wings away up there.
> No. No. don't form dark clouds in my sky this day.

Each line carries so much to unpack, so much that we have to address. How does each image and item corresponds to the overall context unfolding even as more questions arise? We can perhaps gather that the "Bardic Days" refer to those of the speaker and/or the poet, that perhaps the process of what he hopes will illuminate some fertile ground is threatened by an imminent darkness or sadness leaving him (and whoever else is included in the "we") swallowed in a frothy opacity. While this reading definitely requires some elasticity of interpretation, one thing that is clear is that both the speaker's tone and the corresponding mood are as heavy as the lines that carry them, a weight we also feel empathetically as we trudge through the foam and mire. This is further intensified by the fact that the poem is arranged in one big chunk as opposed to individual stanzas. A few breaks between the cluster of lines would interrupt the compact weight of the poem; therefore, keeping all the lines together allows, or better yet forces us, to bear the speaker's burden fully upon our buckling backs (and this is only within the first five lines).

Even as the poem moves in opacity, I'm fascinated by how much Postell allows to be revealed through carefully selected diction. While some words state what is to be felt or seen concretely ("sadness," "crying," "dark clouds"), others, though perhaps unfamiliar at first, gleam with a radiant specificity once their definitions are revealed: *trundel*—to move slowly and heavily; *lambent*—to lick and flicker lightly over the face of a surface. The poem's flickerings between the concrete and abstract, moments of clarity and obscurity, feel as if Postell is recounting the surreal details of a dream—what cannot be illustrated directly is told through bundled approximations, or as the speaker states, "these pick-up trucks of words." This metaphor is perhaps the most significant and resonant in the poem as it seems to confirm the speaker's process for working through the depths of his restlessness.

The contents of what the speaker carries and grapples with often spread and spill out over a series of extended metaphors, complex grammatical structures, and sprawling lines ending in enjambment:

> O lackadaisicallity vibrating
> pedantically over the settlement of these dreams descend
> dumbly to her token heart and stagger through that gloom dying
> like the doubt buried in the plans God made for the unworthy.

Again, Postell pairs precise diction with more abstract and conceptual imagery. In order to best emphasize the meaning and intensity of the word, Postell personifies the adjective "lackadaisical" into an abstract noun. The specificity of the verb "vibrating" and adverb "pedantically" enable us to imagine the intangible: "Lackadaisicallity," the very state of listlessness itself, has somehow found the fervor to pulsate into every detail of where the speaker's dreams reside and come forth. Yet, even as the speaker continues to try to precisely illustrate his frustration over clumsily approaching his beloved's "token heart," he eventually resorts back to surreal comparisons and associations which always yield a more visceral effect.

When I first started reading poetry, one of the first deeply melancholy lines I remember reading was from Poe's brief poem "To\_\_\_\_," in which the speaker, scorned by his lover, states:

> I mourn not that the desolate
> are happier, sweet than I
> But that *you* sorrow for my fate
> Who am a passer by.

The concept of being sadder than the most dejected people in the world not amounting to the pain of being pitied by someone you love cut right to the core of my gloomy little heart. Yet, Postell's ability to conjure up the most strange and novel imagery consistently leaves me feeling a combination of frightened, sad, and intrigued. It scares me to imagine a sadness akin to God burying doubt in my plans, or a hopelessness so deep and grotesque it evokes images of "jack-o-lanterns springing from high places telling dirty jokes," or a darkness likened to "God turned inside-out." Though I may struggle through some of his references at times, it's a privilege to submit to the will of the work, especially in terms of resisting and redressing the expectations that Black poetry should possess a certain transparency of content and form that allows people to feel they have us and our work "figured out." I'm proud to see his work unearthed as a new precedent for possibilities, for the validation of hauling the depths of our imaginations on the page over and over, like a ritual, until we reach something close to what feels right.

# "PIECES OF A MAN": TOM POSTELL, REVENANT

## Aldon Lynn Nielsen

*"anything for a poem"*

It has been the peculiar fate of the name *Tom Postell* to have been not so much unknown or underacknowledged as nearly lost among the fun house mirrors of literary history. To the extent that the American literary world knew Tom Postell at all, it was on the basis of a few fugitive poems, the reminiscences (often obscured by time) of others, and one of the most notorious poems published by Amiri Baraka at the peak of his cultural nationalist period, prior to his conversion to Marxism and his ultimate rejection of all forms of racial and ethnic bigotry.

For many of us, our introduction to Postell's poetry came with the appearance (in my case the much later discovery) of the first issue of the journal *Yugen*, advertising itself as "a new consciousness in arts and letters," edited and published by LeRoi Jones, as Baraka then fashioned his own name, and his wife Hettie Cohen. In the contributors' notes to that issue we read that Postell "came to New York from Cincinnati" and that he had published "previously in *The Naked Ear*, *Virginia Quarterly*, and other magazines." Postell's poetry is found here alongside artists who were to become far better known, such as Philip Whalen, Allen Ginsberg, Baraka himself, and Diane Di Prima, as well as poets who should have become far better known, such as Allen Polite, Stephen Tropp and Bobb Hamilton. He was to appear again in *Yugen 2* with the poem "Harmony," but this time the contributors' note reads simply "Thomas Postell appears again."

But even that early appearance in *Yugen* has occasioned a fair amount of confusion. As the poem appeared in that journal, it bore the title "*Gertrude Stein* Rides the Town Down El," and a dedication "to New York City." When Lauri Scheyer and I wanted to include this poem in our anthology of innovative Black poets of the post-World War II years, we were immediately confronted with the need to make an editorial judgment. We suspected the word "Town" in that title might be a typo. The "W" and "R" are, after all, close neighbors on the QWERTY keyboard, and the final line of the poem speaks of "the torn down El." The journal's Table of Contents turned out to be no help at all. The poem appears there with the title reduced to "Gertrude Stein Rides the El." In the end, lacking access to any manuscript original, we decided to print the poem as it had appeared in *Yugen*. In a fascinating account of a class he taught on the little magazine, Michael Leong takes up this very issue. His students were provided with copies of the poem as it had appeared in *Yugen*, as it had reappeared in our anthology, and as it was presented in Rosemont and Kelly's *Black, Brown, & Beige: Surrealist Writings from Africa and the Diaspora*. Rosemont and Kelly gave yet another version of the title: "Gertrude Stein Rides the Torn Down El to NYC," remaking the poem's dedication as a destination. Their edited version of the poem also removes the indentations in run-over lines, and adds a hyphen in the last line. "Do these differences matter?" That was the question taken up by the class. Of course, any textual scholar will insist that such things matter a great deal. (I still recall a fellow grad student discoursing at some length on the significance of a semicolon in a poem by Robert Frost, which punctuation was indeed an error that had appeared in only one printing of the poem.)

Leong and his students took a fascinating approach to that question. According to him, his group decided that the version that reads "Town Down El," "seems to be Postell's deliberate use of anastrophe . . . the scrambling of syntax [that] parallels Postell's scrambling of time in his anachronistic image of a 'long dead' Stein riding the downtown El" (7). It's a hard observation to argue with, but attributing the oddity to the poet's intention in the absence of a manuscript source is another matter. Scholars attempt to be scrupulous about source texts and the representation of an author's work. Critics, so often the same people, also recognize that a reading of what is actually on the page, regardless of how it got there, is always of interest.

Yet more confusing is the matter of Postell's presence, or the presence of more than one Postell, in *The Autobiography of LeRoi Jones*. In writing of the fourth issue of *Yugen*, Baraka remarks of the presence of "LeRoi Jones" in the issue, that he was the only Black writer in the issue, adding "At the time

I might have thought it was two!" (230) What he is referring to is the poem in that issue by one "Mason Jordan Mason," a "Black" poet who was entirely the invention of the White Judson Crews, who also has poetry in the issue. This sort of racial and identitarian confusion abounds in the literature surrounding Postell and Baraka. Baraka's own name was transfigured by the artist from "Leroy Jones" to "LeRoi Jones," to "Amiri Baraka," and the memoir he published, which itself appeared in two quite different versions, is *The Autobiography of LeRoi Jones* by Amiri Baraka. Small wonder, then, that the memoir further confuses the names of others. Writing his autobiography's first draft during weekends spent in jail, Baraka often adopted pseudonyms for some of the people he had associated with in his life. In the case of Postell, he used both the pseudonym and the real name. In the instance of his mention of *Yugen 4* he uses both names in the same sentence. In this same sentence, he refers to poet and painter Allen Polite by his real name, though elsewhere in the account he is known as "Steve Korret." Here Baraka is listing Black poets who do not appear in later issues of *Yugen*, adding "But I was not socially with them either," marking one stage of his evolution away from his earliest Village experiences. Then, turning to his pseudonym for Postell, he writes: "around that time I had to get Tim out of Bellevue, where one of his drinking bouts had taken him right into the nut ward. I had to testify to his sanity and become his guardian." Such events were not unusual at the time in Baraka's proliferating circles. Beat poet Ray Bremser was also supposedly under Baraka's watchful eye when he was released from prison. In one of the sadder passages regarding Postell, in the midst of contemplating the effects of Malcolm X's words on his own thinking, Baraka thinks about his friend:

wandering down Third Avenue, completely off his rocker. He was mumbling "The Jews are talking through my mouth. The Jews are talking through my mouth." And he tried to clasp his hand across his mouth, spitting these words out as if in terror. The society and the wine had done him in. (274)

We know this is Postell, hidden behind the moniker "Tim Poston," because precisely the same event is invoked in what is perhaps Baraka's most notoriously anti-Semitic poem, "For Tom Postell, Dead Black Poet," a poem most certainly not included in Baraka's final volume of selected poems, *SOS: Poems 1961–2013.* Nor, mercifully, was it to be found in any of his earlier selected volumes, dating back to 1979's *Selected Poems.* That volume was his first full length selected, and it was the first to be published following his conversion to Marxism and total rejection of cultural nationalism. The book in which "For Tom Postell" was published was itself a sort of selected. *Black Magic Poetry 1961–1967* was described on its title page as "collected poetry," and was divided into three sections: "Sabotage," "Target Study" and "Black Art." The book traces Baraka's development from *The Dead Lecturer* into the years of his Black Arts work. "For Tom Postell" is found in the third section of that book, "Black Art," and registers the movement into the nationalist phase, and into the poet's new name, though here it is spelled "Ameer Baraka." In his prefatory notes to the book, the poet writes "I leave this poetry at 1966 because I did not want to give the devils all of it" (np).

Because so little was known of Postell in the American literary world in the years since, this poem has become inevitably linked to his name. "The jews are talking through my mouth," the poem repeats, many years before the same scene is narrated in Baraka's autobiography. So this poem becomes the always to be recited evidence against Baraka;

justly so. As I've said in the past, it is not a particularly good defense against charges of anti-Semitism to say that a poet *used to be* a bigot but has transformed himself into an anti-bigotry egalitarian. Postell himself is not available to speak to his manifestation in Baraka's poem, to narrate, possibly, his own redemption.

Baraka's poem opens: "You told me, you told me / a thousand years ago" (153). Baraka then chided himself for not attending to Postell's drinking, to mental instability. "Only the winebottles lived / and sparkled and sailed easily for completion" (153), Baraka observes, drinking right alongside his poet friend. (Little has been written to date about these poems from the early decades that speak of communal addling of consciousness.) "I didn't hear / you brother." But Baraka does here credit Postell's enormous influence on his own development as an artist. "I wallowed in your intestines, / brother, stole, and changed, your poems." Hard to tell in these lines if Baraka is speaking of his own poetry's reliance upon Postell's influence, or, perhaps more likely, his editorial interventions in Postell's published works. In the autobiography, as Baraka recollects the founding of *Yugen*, he notes that several of his young Black poet friends had not published much. In Baraka's own case, he chalked lack of publication at that point up to rejections; he doesn't speculate about why Postell may not have published more.

As Baraka moves into the second part of his poem for Postell, the anti-Semitism becomes yet more violent, and more personal. "Why they hate me" he notes, speaking specifically about Martin Duberman, who would later publish a major history of Black Mountain College. Baraka spoke often of the Black Mountain influences in his work, and among his early friendships. But Duberman had argued in an essay in 1966,

"James Meredith and LeRoi Jones," that Baraka was more fixed upon achieving a private catharsis than upon any actual communication, precisely the sort of unthinking criticism so often leveled at innovative poetry. That Baraka associates Duberman's cliched reading to his ethnicity is just one sign of his own warped thinking at the time. Still, while there is utterly no justification for the vile things said in this poem, it remains a poem often misread. Just what is it that Baraka says he has in store for Jews? "I got this thing, goes pulsating through black everything / universal meaning" (154). And when he speaks of "the extermination blues," what he says Hitler couldn't stand was the Jews' "closeness to the truth." It is at once, ultimately, an incoherent rant and a racist rant. The Marxist Baraka has never reprinted it in a book, nor has he, so far as I know, ever included the poem in any readings after about 1970. It remains an unforgivable moment. It is difficult at this distance to know how much Postell's own thoughts aligned with this. On the evidence of Baraka's poem and autobiography, the Postell of late breakdown had been suggesting such thoughts to Baraka before Baraka himself had moved fully into the intolerance of that period of his work. Would Postell have distanced himself from such thoughts in a later life as Baraka eventually did?

What we do know is the poetry Postell left behind, the poetry recovered and published in this gathering. In a poem titled "Poem" in this volume, Postell states starkly "I hate Ezra Pound." Pound was still very much alive at the time of this poem's writing, and was only released from Saint Elizabeth's hospital in 1958. His influence on the prosody of the New American Poetry was inescapable. We do know Postell had read Pound closely enough to borrow from him. Here we have the poem "I Make A Pact With You LeRoi

Jones I Have Ignored You Long Enough," a poem that mimics Pound's "Pact" in which he reconciles himself with the ineluctable influence of Walt Whitman. Pound's own racism was tightly bound up with his anti-Semitism, and African American poets responding to Modernism's impulses had somehow to negotiate their way through that morass. In the case of a Stephen Jonas, the result was poetry that was often as violently anti-Jewish as anything in Pound, or in Baraka. Though Postell was a poet already on the scene when Baraka arrived, and one who exercised influence over the young LeRoi Jones, the relationship had not always been an easy one. Both Postell and Baraka were, to say the very least, often difficult friends. In the poem "Poem" Postell mentions "telegrams from LeRoi Jones to the judge," presumably a reference to the time spoken of in Baraka's *Autobiography* when he had interceded on Postell's behalf. And in the poetry we see that Postell was wrestling with many of the same racial issues in the communities that he and Baraka inhabited in the early sixties. Another poem begins:

> boy
> you thought you were white
> something we never dreamed of
> now you say you are whole
> now you realize you are black
> —black maybe
> you are telling white people
> now you have seen the light
> still waiting for them to pat your back

This piece reflects the kinds of racial situations that were increasingly roiling the communities of Black poets in those years rolling into the Black Arts era.

Had Postell ever actually ignored LeRoi Jones? Is it Postell's own songs that he describes as having "gone to use burned in fires of rejection slips," lines that echo Baraka's retrospective comments about the publication opportunities afforded these young tyros within even the more bohemian communities of past-WWII arts. "This poem was blended in Scotland and bottled in Cincinnati / But you can open it when you please, and you can go to hell too." It would be worth knowing at just which stage of the two poets' relationship this was written. A clear allusion to drinking problems (also the poem's final reference to scotch and scotch tape), seemingly associated with his Ohio background, at the same time reflecting some sort of tensions between poet/editor Baraka and the struggling Postell. The poem, as is true of most of Postell's work, proceeds in accord with the postmodern poetics of Black Mountain influenced artists. Poets of that era seemed obsessed with, without ever really coming to ready conclusions, measure. In the wake of Williams's attempts to define a variable foot, poets such as Creeley, Baraka, George Stanley, Duncan and Wieners constantly spoke of an organic measure that was an extension of content, that was to emerge in the act of composition itself. A sort of ironic revenge of literary history, then, finds the title of John Wieners's poetry magazine *Measure* replicated today as the name of a journal of formal verse. In his "pact" with Baraka, a poet in his early years much given to expatiating on the prosody of the New American Poetry, Postell writes: "— mean measures, rhythms catch and hold, gathered days gather / gone lines . . ." And readers of Baraka's work, or Olson's, will recognize the principles at work in a composition such as this one: one perception moving, as Olson put it, "instanter" on another. Open form, but with emphasis upon sound. The typed poem as a sort of score for its reading. Tom Postell was already *there* when he met Baraka, and, at least early on, the two of them were pursuing what would soon be seen as the major stream of innovative poetics in America.

Then, too, one reason Postell had not published more was race. Donald Allen only found room for one Black poet in *The New American Poetry*, and had it not been for the friendship between Frank O'Hara and Baraka, there might well have been none. Baraka was from the outset a proponent of the DIY aesthetic. Knowing that much of his work would never be welcome in such venues as the *New Yorker*, he initiated publishing projects with other like-minded artists, ventures such as *Yugen*, where Postell appeared twice, *Floating Bear*, *Totem/Corinth Press* and others. Postell was not one to build institutions, and remained largely at the mercy of editors, who, face it, were in those days mostly White people.

There are many more light-hearted moments in Postell, such as his take down of Joyce Kilmer: "I would like to write a poem / more beautiful than a tree / and sell it to a dog." And then there are moments of sharp self-recognition: "Once I was sober / as a fox in a refrigerator / three weeks and twice as anti-social." Even here, though, that moment of reckoning with his own demons is lifted into another degree of rhetoric by that sharp and striking image of a fox in a fridge. In "WXYZ" (the title completes an alphabet begun in the body of the poem), the poet who avows at the outset "anything for a poem" turns out to have one red line. "But not virtue I'll not give up this virtue you can plainly see." Everything else may have fallen away from Tom Postell as he himself was failing, but there was a remnant of integrity he would never abandon, not even for a poem.

In the end, there is something both prophetic and tragic about this passage in Postell's "Pact": "words unstring me!"

Any poet struggling to create will recognize the sentiment, but, to judge from Baraka's memories of Postell, the phrase took on a more literal significance as his poet friend slid into illness and obscurity. We speak of stringing words together, but what was strung can always be unstrung. Perhaps with the almost too late recovery of the poems of Tom Postell, the unsung can finally find voice.

## WORKS CITED

Baraka, Amiri. *The Autobiography of LeRoi Jones.* Chicago: Lawrence Hill Books, 1997.

—. *Black Magis Poetry 1961–1967.* New York: Bobbs Merril, 1969.

Leong, Michael. *Teaching the Little Magazine.* The Poetry Collection of the University Libraries, SUNY Buffalo. Among the Neighbors 10, 2019.

Postell, Tom. *Poems from the Tomb.*" 75.

*Yugen.* LeRoi Jones and Hettie Cohen, Eds. New York: 1958.

# FOUR SCORES
# (FOR AND AFTER TOM POSTELL)

## giovanni singleton

The following "scores," as I am calling them, attempt to engage what I sense as an "ongoingness" and/or "beingness" in Postell's work. This comes through in his surrealist leanings and his use of -ing. Three of the four scores are built around verbs, nouns, gerunds, prepositions, adjectives, etc. that appear in Postell's poems. They are their own kind of unending music.

*score no. 1*

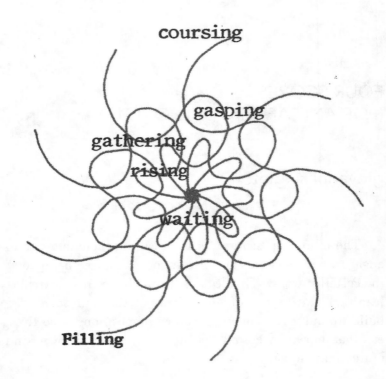

score no. 2

## score no. 3

Eating Eating
Laughing Laughing
chewing chewing
grinning grinning
Swallowing Swallowing
unsuspecting unsuspecting
Appreciating Appreciating
Taking Taking
rotting rotting
laughing laughing
Dancing Dancing

score no. 4

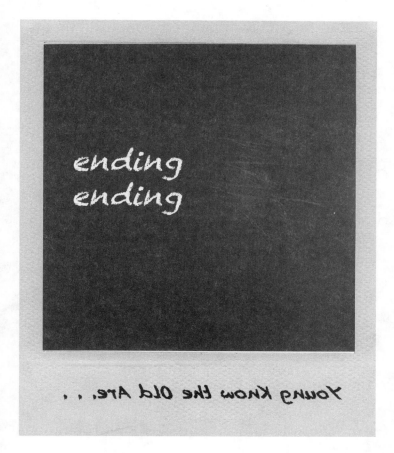

# OPUS THREADS 1 & 2

dior j. stephens

What does a dolphin wish for? What does a black
dolphin wish for? What does a black dolphin from a
son of a homemaker and pullman porter wish for?
If we are to think of, imagine, wishing as a political
gesture, we must also think of what it means for a man
(a dolphin) like Postell to venture towards a wish

The politics of Postell's era, much like our own, were
not kind to Postell and his kin. In 1950, Dr. Ralph
Bunche becomes the first Black Nobel Peace Prize
Winner for his work in mediating the Arab-Isreali war of
1947-1949. Postell would have been just seventeen
years old at the time of this historic landmark
Bunche—a Midwesterner from humble roots, like
Postell—wished and fought for a lasting peace in the
Middle East. There's stories of Bunche commissioning
a local potter to craft commemorative plates for the
representatives of the prolonged, arduous talks well
before it was clear that the talks would be a success
It is written that, when asked what Bunche would've
done if the negations had failed, he responded "I'd
have broken the plates over your damn heads."

Surely then, to wish, as a Black man, as any
marginalized body living in the shadow of empire
is not only a political gesture but a radical motion
towards true freedom and the right of self-agency
A right, as Postell witnessed as he became an adult
in the revolutionary midsts of the Civil Rights Era, that
the superstructure of the United States insists is no
self-evident nor endowed with any unalienable rights
Rights must be fought for, defended, dreamed of, and
for poets like Postell, deeply, recurrently wished for

In his poem "I Want a Solid Piece of Sunlight and a
Yardstick to Measure It With," Postell paints the

picture of New York City's Seventh Avenue at midday.
Unpleasant with "a gray tide of suits [coming] out
for air" and "brown buildings [dripping] with wilting
plaster," Postell illustrates "the redundant oasis" of the
United States (and of its unofficial cultural-capital city).
Redundant, here, feels entirely exacting in its labeling.

Redundant, as an adjective, can mean "not or no
longer needed or useful; superfluous." Apart from
being an exceptional read, attributing the US to a
"redundant oasis" casts a marvelous lens on the
rhinestoned cacophony that is the United States of
America (and the profound irony of existing in it
as a resplendent black body).

Later in the piece, Postell returns to his wish, pleading:
"O give me a solid piece of sunlight and a yardstick of
my own and the right to holler." Solid as in legitimate;
real. Sunlight as in iridescent; luminous. Yardstick
as in measurable; exacting. Yet, I'd argue most
importantly, is the "right to holler" as in: the right to
scream, cry, yell, twist, shout (out against an empire
that constantly, consistently seeks to silence you).

Postell's wishing, in this way, is not only a political
gesture but a gesture towards Black Futurity. An
imagined space (an essential, spiritual space) of the
freedom Postell writes towards in so much of his work.
There's a palpable longing that shouts from the
depths of Postell's spirit that both captivates and
sorrows the soul, for, in so many unfortunate ways, I
see our people, our Black dolphin pod, striving and
reaching for those very same wishes.

What does a dolphin wish for? They wish for peace,
safety, and the constant comfort of being in the
presence of their people. If dolphin is tradition then it
is to be in a tradition of wishing for a futurity of
freedom… for Blacks in the USA, for Palestinians
in Gaza, for every and all bodies that are targeted
by the State. Postell wished in the dolphin tradition.
Dr. Ralph Bunche wished in the dolphin tradition.
How wild, that wishing, that lineage of wishing.
How wilder still that it has not come to an end.

ta Maria della Salute,

ll like this eternal doomsday

ing me

u idea who I am now, do you not

ig

t

dolphin drifting thru the west

there's a scene in a movie i've never seen but somehow ingrained in my mind. 1969's "midnight cowboy." dustin hoffman, jon voight. a naive cowboy from texas and a con-man in new york city.

scene goes a little something like this:

ratso (hoffman) is going off on joe (voight) on some rant about the importance of middlemen in his con-artist operations.

they're strolling down a jam-packed manhattan sidewalk, blithely walking into an intersection, a yellow cab screeches to halt in the c r o s s w a l k .

ratso (hoffman) shouts at the driver, **"hey!"** *slams cab hood, twice* **"i'm walking here! i'm walking here!"**

*it is precisely that ferocity within the (privilege-stained) tenor of hoffman's voice that stays with me the most.*

*ratso (what a name) is asserting his right to* **be** *and to be absolutely whatever wherever the hell he wants.*

*but it was actually just the voice that stuck with me. in fact, i had misremembered the language of the scene altogether. in my mind the shout went:*

**hey! i'm talking to you! i'm talking to you!**

*dolphins, like humans, have a syncopated heartbeat. as highly intelligent (occasionally mischievous) mammals, one might surmise that dolphins are also deeply attuned to i n t i m a c y .*

*they form pods; stick together. they mate freely and in non-monogamous partnerships.*

*one might even argue that dolphins are capable of longing, or even desire.*

*it's less of a reach to gleam that postell was of the poetic tradition of longing, wishing, and desire. minds like Postell's, that grow up through intertwined nets of disenfranchisement and marginalization, are all too familiar with the infinite ways in which they are silenced... by institutions, by governments, by the status quo.*

*black avant-garde poets are deeply attuned to this plight.*

*while discussing this writing with an editor of this book, m.c.peterson, we fell upon a philosophical debate on whether or not poets are trying to close or elongate the distance between reader and poet.*

*some poets are looking to close that distance. some poets want you to swim with them in their pod of poetic thought, longing, and feeling. some don t.*

*this tightrope-thin line has been walked by poets since the since before since. for poets like Postell, this intimacy divide (/chasm/schism/break/rift/) can be viewed as a threat that sows something much more sinister than mere distance.*

*if we, as readers, distance ourselves from the (dolphin) hearts of poets like Postell, we run the risk of distancing ourselves from narratives that paint some of the truest portraits of black, marginalized (check: silenced) life in the united states.*

kissing bug

loud night

my kit of mornings

dolphin of my hear

Postell was, perhaps, the defiant ratso of his time. slamming
against the hood of america and asserting his "right to holler."

or, in his words, from his poem "amoeboid," to be

"the that that is."

like ratso/hoffman, Postell too, is angling for the right to be
(safe, loud, alive, vibrant).

writers like Postell seek to close the poetic distance between
reader and the dolphin of their heart to disturb, jar, unnerve
readers into the orbit of a life.

ly tucked away

*some poets are talking to you here*
*some poets are talking to you here*
*some poets are talking to you here*

*some poets are talking to you here*
*some poets are talking to you here*
*some poets are talking to you here*
*some poets are talking to you here*

# CONTRIBUTORS

brittny ray crowell (she/her/hers) is an Assistant
Professor of English at Clark Atlanta University. A
recipient of a Donald Barthelme Prize in Poetry and the
Lucy Terry Prince Prize, her poems have appeared in
*Copper Nickel*, *Ploughshares*, and elsewhere. Her work as a
librettist has been featured at Ohio State University and
the Kennedy Center's *Cartography Project*. Her current
research focuses on personal archives and intuitive
witness in the work of Black women poets in addition to
food traditions and rituals in Black culture.

DERRICK HARRIELL is Professor of English and Creative
Writing at the University of Wisconsin-Milwaukee.
His previous collections of poems include *Stripper in
Wonderland*, *Come Kingdom*, *Cotton*, and *Ropes*, winner of the
2014 Mississippi Institute of Arts and Letters Poetry Book
Award. His short story, "There's a Riot Goin' On," was
the recipient of the Robert L. Fish Memorial Award. He
holds an MFA from Chicago State University and a Ph.D.
from the University of Wisconsin-Milwaukee. His essays
have been published widely.

ALDON LYNN NIELSEN is the Kelly Professor of American Literature at Penn State University. He was the first winner of the Larry Neal Award for poetry. His recent books include *The Inside Songs of Amiri Baraka*, *Back Pages: Selected Poems*, *Spider Cone* and *Meme Wars*.

MICHAEL C. PETERSON is Assistant Professor and Curator of the Elliston Poetry Collection and Audio Archive at the University of Cincinnati, where Tom Postell's papers newly reside. A recipient of fellowships from MacDowell, Yaddo, Kenyon Writers' Workshop, and the Vermont Studio Center, his poems have appeared in journals such as *Fence*, *Boston Review Online*, *Southern Review*, *Blackbird*, *Gulf Coast*, *New American Writing*, and elsewhere. His work has been anthologized in *Of Rivers: Poets Respond to Langston Hughes* and *They Said: A Multi-Genre Anthology of Contemporary Collaborative Writing*. He holds degrees from Stanford University, UVA, the University of North Carolina-Greensboro, and a doctorate from the University of Cincinnati.

singleton, geovanni

giovanni singleton is the author of *Ascension*, informed by the life and work of Alice Coltrane, which won the California Book Award Gold Medal, and the visual art collection *AMERICAN LETTERS: works on paper*. Founding editor of *nocturnes (re)view of the literary arts*, singleton is the recipient of the African American Literature and Culture Society's Stephen E. Henderson Award for Outstanding Achievement in Poetry.

stephens, dior j.

dior j. stephens is a proud Pisces hailing from Lake Erie. He is the author of the chapbooks *SCREAMS & lavender*, *001*, and *CANNON!* Their debut full-length collection, *CRUEL/CRUEL*, is out now with Nightboat Books. A Cave Canem, Lambda Literary, and Sewanee fellow, they happily serve as the Managing Poetry Editor of *Foglifter Journal* and Press. You can find their work in journals like *HaveHasHad*, *Peach Mag*, *Somesuch Stories*, and *fourteen poems*, among others. They exist online on Instagram @dolphinphotos and Twitter @dolphinneptune

SUTTON, ANTHONY

ANTHONY SUTTON resides on former Akokisas, Atakapa, Karankawa, and Sana land (currently named Houston, TX), as an Inprint C. Glenn Cambor fellow at the University of Houston's Creative Writing and Literature PhD program. Winner of the 2024 Inprint Marion Barthelme Prize in Creative Writing and author of the poetry collection *Particles of a Stranger Light* (Veliz Books, 2023), Anthony's poetry has appeared or if forthcoming in *Grist, guesthouse, Gulf Coast, Prairie Schooner, Oversound, Quarter After Eight, Texas Review, Zone 3*, the anthology *In the Tempered Dark: Contemporary Poets Transcending Elegy*, and elsewhere.

# ACKNOWLEDGEMENTS

The Editors wish to extend their gratitude foremostly to Rose Bianchi, Katherine Jones, Beverly Miller, and the entire Postell Family: your knowledge, wisdom, and time have been an immeasurable gift to us. Rose Bianchi dutifully kept the fire of these manuscripts for over four decades; as such, her expertise in their origins and composition has been the very fundament of any investigation we've undertaken. Katherine Jones and daughter Beverly Miller remain the firmament of family for us, their knowledge and spirit being the crucial ethical voice of this volume. Their artistry with and wisdom of broader constellations of Cincinnati musical and cultural folkways is the beating heart of this endeavor. Katherine: you have fed us with your warmth, wit, patience, and freshly-cut fruit to keep us going. This volume would not have been possible without Beverly Miller's assistance in all matters genealogical and the search for long-thought-lost documentation. There is no gratitude enough for your friendship in this process. We are likewise indebted to Claudette Fikes, who worked quickly to locate rare photographs and share them with the team.

In addition to thanking Directors Wayne Miller, Kevin Prufer, and Martin Rock, we would like to thank the entire Unsung Masters Series Board for their vision, advocacy, critical eye, and fellowship: Kazim Ali, Sarah Ehlers, Niki Herd, Benjamin Johnson, Joanna Luloff, Jenny Molberg, and Adrienne Perry. Special thanks must be expressed to Series Co-Editor Kevin Prufer, who has been a tireless advocate of the work herein and a maestro of editorial counsel. Poet, designer, and meticulous editor Martin Rock has made Tom's poems truly sing on these pages, solving for their challenging typographical riffs with dexterity, sagacity, and forbearance.

Immense gratitude is due to the contributors of this volume—brittny ray crowell, Derrick Harriell, Aldon Lynn Nielsen, giovanni singleton, and dior j. stevens—who jumped faithfully into dialogue with the mystery of Tom's work, compositions that few had ever seen up to now. You have been this volume's unwavering rhythm section, generous of your time, artistry, and spirit to make the volume's melody rich in the listening. We are in abiding awe of your inspired playing. To quote Cecil Taylor, our words are always inadequate to describe your music.

Friends, family, and colleagues lent their support and compass to this volume behind the scenes, listening to poems, weighing in, or otherwise pointing us in good direction: Don Bogen, Haylee Harrell, francine j. harris, Aditi Machado, Catherine Niu, Katie Peterson, Heather Williams, Felicia Zamora, and Jacob Zimmerman. Your input has been pure artistry. We also wish to acknowledge Jenefer Robinson and Jay Twomey, key liaisons to our rendezvous with Tom.

Finally, our curation of Tom Postell's work has been deeply enriched by the knowledge of community members, jazz-players, photographers, and journalists who have given of their time to help better draw Tom's figure in the era: Amy Culbertson, Melvin Grier, Lou Lausche, Jack Wilkins, Jon Hughes, Ron Enyard, Paul Gibby, Stephen Marine, Brian Kelly, and Brent Gallaher. We count ourselves fortunate to know your stories, and hope the conversation continues.

THIS EDITION OF THE UNSUNG MASTERS
IS PRODUCED AS A COLLABORATION AMONG:

*Gulf Coast: A Journal of Literature and Fine Arts*
and
*Copper Nickel*
and
*Pleiades: Literature in Context*


GENEROUS SUPPORT AND FUNDING PROVIDED BY:

University of Houston Department of English


This book is set in Marion with Avenir
essay titles and Poiret One page numbers.